Successful Sons Psychotherapeutic Guide for Parents

Psychotherapeutic Principles for Success and Happiness, Volume 1

Ylich Tarazona

Published by Ylich Eduard Tarazona Gil, 2023.

SUCCESSFUL SONS PSYCHOTHERAPEUTIC GUIDE FOR PARENTS

First edition. February 8, 2023.

ISBN: 979-8215637234

Written by Ylich Tarazona.

Table of Contents

DEDICATION.

Dedicated especially for you, my dear reader...

May this book provide you with the tools you need to start teaching, educating, and raising your children in an extraordinary way.

Discover the power of this guide, which will help empower you to be the best parent you can be. With our easy-to-follow program, you will learn how to raise your children with respect and love while communicating clear and precise expectations for children to understand, all while promoting positive principles and values at home. You will also receive practical advice on how to teach ethics, morals and good manners that will stick with your children for life.

Providing you with the bridge, the right vehicle and the inspiration to create, carve and build a better destiny for all the members of the family nucleus...

Your Great Friend **YLICH TARAZONA.**

DEDICATION

Successful Sons

Psychotherapeutic Guide for Parents

A guide that will teach us in a simple way how to educate and raise our children in a balanced and integral way.

This book is the definitive guide for parents who want to learn how to teach their children in a positive environment for their full development and formation. It provides step-by-step instructions and practical advice on how to establish a healthy environment for homeschooling centered on principles and values.

In addition, it provides simple and effective strategies and a variety of psychotherapeutic tools that parents will need to create a nurturing and supportive environment that will help them raise and educate their children more effectively.

"Successful Children" is an invaluable psychotherapeutic guide for parents, providing simple and effective strategies for raising and educating children in a healthy and positive way. It is an essential resource for any parent seeking to create a loving and supportive environment.

This book provides an easy-to-follow guide on how to raise, educate and teach children. It offers practical advice on how to foster healthy and successful relationships with your children. It also provides an overview of the most effective psychotherapeutic approaches to parenting in the 21st century.

In conclusion, parenting can be a difficult and challenging task. However, by understanding the basic principles and values of parenting, parents can not only create a loving home environment, but also help their children become successful adults. With the right tools and guidance, parents can learn how to guide their children effectively to make choices that will benefit them eventually.

By practicing these psychotherapeutic tips, parents can ensure that their children will become strong, independent individuals with a healthy set of values.

Series: ***Psychotherapeutic Principles for Success and Happiness***

1st Special Edition, revised, updated, and extended.

(Includes practical exercises and action plan).

Written by YLICH TARAZONA.

Writer and International Speaker.

COPYRIGHT.

This work, ***"SUCCESSFUL SONS – Psychotherapeutic Guide for Parents. A guide that will teach us in a simple way how to educate and raise our children in a balanced and integral way*** © ®". It is intellectual property of Ylich Tarazona.

Date of Publication: 7-February-2023 – 20:33 UTC.

Disclaimer of Liability

Every effort has been made to make this report as complete, up-to-date, and accurate as possible, up to the date of publication. However, it may lack some ideas to expand and improve the content; or, in its effect, contain some topics that it is advisable to study more about them.

The purpose of this book is only to educate and provide information of value to the reader. The author and publisher do not guarantee that the information contained in this book is completely accurate, as these are points that are being researched and new studies are appearing every day. For our part, the current content we share with our readers is current as of the date of publication.

The author and publisher shall have no liability or responsibility to any person or entity regarding any situation caused directly or indirectly by the misuse of this book. Therefore, readers are invited to take the information with good judgment. And take our content, for what it is, as advice, a support, an alternative, valuable information; and in no case take it as an unequivocal solution.

DEDICATION.

Dedicated especially for you, my dear reader...

May this book provide you with the tools you need to start teaching, educating, and raising your children in an extraordinary way.

Discover the power of this guide, which will help empower you to be the best parent you can be. With our easy-to-follow program, you will learn how to raise your children with respect and love while communicating clear and precise expectations for children to understand, all while promoting positive principles and values at home. You will also receive practical advice on how to teach ethics, morals and good manners that will stick with your children for life.

Providing you with the bridge, the right vehicle and the inspiration to create, carve and build a better destiny for all the members of the family nucleus...

Your Great Friend **YLICH TARAZONA.**

INTRODUCTION

With the purpose of orienting parents interested in the adequate and balanced behavioral formation of their children, I wish to express, through this guide for parents. My desire to share my life experience as a husband and father of a family. I would also like to share part of my professional trajectory as a family psychotherapist and mental health specialist.

This sort of life lesson to share with you, is drawn from my challenges, as well as my successes, from my failures and my mistakes, from trial and error, and finally from my learning throughout this process.

This information, both personal and professional, which I will share with you, is intended to help you in the great task of forming the "citizens of the future", your extraordinary children.

This work is addressed to responsible parents and, to all those who are thinking of becoming parents of future generations, those children, young people and adolescents who will be integrated as potential drivers of the society and the world of tomorrow.

It is important to emphasize that: No one studies to be a parent and, when we take on this vital challenge, sometimes, we must do it with what we know so far and have within reach. And even, sometimes, we must update ourselves in the face of new online trends and digital technologies. And thus, give our children a more comprehensive education that prepares them to take on the challenges of tomorrow.

This information is based not only on ethical, moral and spiritual principles centered within the home, which is the first school of life. It also focuses on teaching our children to learn to socialize and interact responsibly and respectfully with all people.

✓ ***To love** is not to overindulge children, nor to please them in everything they ask for.*

✓ ***To love*** *is to care for and protect them with care, to lead them along the tender paths of love, good behavior, respect, and obedience.*

✓ ***To love*** *is to instill in them with wisdom and a lot of strength the desire to learn from our experience, so that, in the future, they will reach their goals as well-formed men and women.*

✓ ***To love*** *is to teach our children principles and values that help them forge a balanced and healthy character, emotionally and psychologically.*

Homeschooling is and always will be a parent's responsibility to help their children achieve their highest purpose and help them, in turn, learn to face the challenges to come.

While it is true that modernity has brought us digital technology, accelerating the processes of personal management in the education of our children. It is also true that the traditional teaching and habits, imparted within the bond of the home, are and will always be extremely necessary for the correct formation of a child.

Let us keep in mind that, as parents, we have the opportunity to contribute to creating a better society. By learning to be parents with freedom of thought, judgment, feelings, imagination, and love for our children, we can continue to be, as far as possible, builders of a better future for future generations.

This guide to raising successful children has the primary objective of encouraging parents to become aware of what they have in their hands: extraordinary human beings, offspring of their lineage, ready to be shapers of the new world.

So fathers and mothers together, let's make our children become the best versions of themselves that they can BE.

So, without further ado – let's get started....

I WILL LEARN IN THIS GUIDE FOR PARENTS

How to foster an effective relationship with your child and develop strong communication skills, mutual trust and respect in the home, which are essential to raising children who have self-confidence and a healthy sense of self.

You will learn how to establish discipline: Discipline is an important part of raising children, but it can be a difficult challenge to know when to draw the line. For that reason, this guide will help you understand the best way to discipline your children correctly while still providing emotional support. And thus, develop clear expectations and boundaries that will help children understand their duties and responsibilities at home, helping them become responsible adults.

Learn how to build confidence in your children: Knowing how to raise a confident child is one of the most difficult tasks for any parent. With psychotherapeutic guidance, you'll get practical tips for developing your child's self-esteem and self-image through recognition of their achievements, sincere praise and words of encouragement that will help your children overcome the challenges they may face along the way.

Learn how to teach principles and values: Every family has unique values they want to instill in their children, yet occasionally, it can be difficult to know where to start. This parenting guide offers guidance on how to teach principles and values such as honesty, integrity, kindness, respect, and communication in easy-to-follow steps that will help shape your children's outlook on life, building successful children.

You will learn to increase your parenting skills: With this psychotherapeutic guide, parents will gain the tools necessary to understand their children and develop a strong relationship based on trust, respect and clear communication. As a result, parents will be better equipped to guide their children in the right direction.

You will learn the basic elements of education: This guide provides information on the basic elements of education, such as self-control, respect for others, proper discipline, and understanding how to form meaningful relationships with children.

Learn how to strengthen family bonds: This psychotherapeutic guide teaches parents how to create a safe environment that is conducive to building strong family bonds. It focuses on establishing an emotional connection between parents and children through positive reinforcement and effective communication strategies.

Learn how to prevent problem behaviors: Parents can use the strategies in this guide to identify potential problems before they arise, as well as provide guidance when they do occur in a more effective way. Understanding your child's needs and responding appropriately to them can help prevent difficult behaviors in the future.

You will learn how to become a role model: This guide helps parents learn how to become role models for their children by showing them the importance of living centered on principles and values such as honesty, integrity, responsibility, empathy and kindness, all of which are essential elements in forming successful members of society.

Learn to communicate with your child: This psychotherapeutic guide provides parents with the essential tools to understand and communicate effectively with their children. Offering simple methods to foster a meaningful parent-child connection based on mutual respect, trust, and understanding.

Learn how to develop an authentic home environment: This psychotherapeutic guide teaches parents how to create healthy boundaries within family bonds and establish an environment of positivity. It also offers tips on how to develop strong communication skills and problem-solving skills that will result in healthier relationships between children, their families, and their environment.

You will learn how to raise confident and responsible children: This psychotherapeutic guide for parents will help you raise confident children with strong values who can make responsible decisions in life. You will learn how to identify your child's unique needs, develop their strengths, encourage them to take risks, solve problems independently and become self-sufficient adults.

Learn to build lasting connections: This psychotherapeutic guide encourages parents to build lasting connections with their children by establishing consistent routines, engaging in meaningful conversations, setting clear behavioral expectations, encouraging independent thinking, active listening, expressing unconditional love and mutual understanding, among others.

You will learn how to nurture your children's character: This psychotherapeutic guide for parents provides valuable information on how to raise children with strong morals and behavioral standards. Using techniques such as positive reinforcement, modeling desirable behavior, providing feedback and guidance, celebrating successes and achievements, this guide will also help you nurture your children's character in the best possible way.

ARE WE READY TO BE PARENTS?

Reaching a level of physical, emotional, mental, and psychological maturity is the condition that ensures that children will grow up healthy and strong in all aspects of their lives. I do not pretend to be perfect, and even less to believe that I know everything related to the care, upbringing, education, training, and development of children, youth, and adolescents.

However, I do wish to share my professional experience as a psychotherapist, as well as some relevant insights and information on the subject, to make the parental task easier.

And thus, learn to give our children, the guidelines of a good formation, as of all those who in the future will form the generations that will continue to sustain the world of today.

Children can sometimes confuse us with many questions and, if we do not know how to answer them at that moment, it will be our personal conscience that, through experience and the advance of time, will answer these questions.

Considering that each one of us is a world, when we reach the possibility of procreating, we will have to self-analyze, prepare ourselves and even organize ourselves to receive the offspring, product of our conjugal union. This will be the enormous mission and responsibility of many years, and not a simple emotional passing task.

As parents, we will have to draw on our empirical and even scientific and psychological knowledge to make this world a sensitive and beautiful place. Capable of making our children the leaders of a society that is moving towards integral development.

In conclusion, parents, relatives, teachers, and society in general are together in this action, which receives the help of technological advances and new psycho-pedagogical concepts. Above all, of the principles and values that must always prevail in those who, as infants in formation, are our sole and total responsibility.

THE FAMILY NUCLEUS

With the passing of time, the family continues to have an absolute value for all human beings. The family is susceptible to constant changes to adapt gradually and progressively to new situations arising from the dizzying stages of economic, social and cultural progress.

That is why, every day, the family must take on new challenges and, to do so, it will even have to accept new roles in life.

As a basic institution of society, the family nucleus fulfills an educative task within the value of righteousness and challenges of modernity.

This educational work will be adapted to the characterization and mimicry of the children within the family.

As parents, we are and will be a continuous example for our children, no matter how complex the concept of parenthood is, which is nothing more than educating them with love, dedication, understanding, and stimuli that form their character and personality.

The experience of parenthood is acquired to the extent that parents know the primary needs of their children.

To raise children with principles and values is to forge loving children with their parents, firm in conduct, character and with future projection.

The primordial base is to dedicate them a space to fill their days and, incidentally, the blank "hard disk" with which they are born. We, as parents, must take care of programming it correctly, nourishing it with relevant information for its formation, all centered on the standards of ethics and good moral habits.

This is the only way to mold a useful, truthful, honest, supportive and happy human being in society; a being who is determined to be a good son, a loyal brother, a responsible father and an excellent leader and head of the family nucleus in the future.

Parenting is not easy nowadays. With the work schedule and the responsibility of household chores, the absence of both parents causes psycho-emotional imbalances in children.

As it is our job to be attentive to their education, it is convenient that parents become more involved in the life and needs of the little ones. We must learn to interpret their cries, their problems, and, above all, to know the concerns that they cannot express through the complex body language and non-verbal communication of the little one.

The objective is to ensure that children in the formative stage-manage to live a happy, full and pleasant time. Not only with a view to a planned and balanced instructional and pedagogical result, but also with a view to the future of their careers.

Natality is the psycho-emotional development, it is a primordial step in its evolutionary stage. This is achieved by consciously exercising the application of knowledge achieved by parents in the "university of life" and the constant training and learning that prepares them, more and more, to offer a better education to their children.

The role of the mother is important and vital in the upbringing of children during the first years of their lives, since the formation of the personality, character, and behavior of their successors depends on it.

It is essential to provide educational and formative resources to promote in children attitudes and aptitudes that will help them in their growth and development, as well as moral values and soft skills through didactic games, sports, art, music, singing, dancing, among others.

The development of the child's personality involves the challenges within the innovative, formal education and in accordance with the evolutionary phases of the person. I make regular reference to parents, since they are the ones who should act as formers of determined human beings; and, provide a good upbringing, procure a healthy life and a healthy, nutritious and balanced diet for their children.

During the first years of life, parents should assume important roles as socializing agents for their children, and give them everything they need to turn them into prepared people. Human beings socially adapted to the changes of the world, the same that needs thinking and active beings. That is to say, social entities.

Every human being is born with individual innate biological and psychological capacities. Therefore, learning to know and enhance their intelligence requires a lot of effort and perseverance.

As a consequence of the affective, communicative, informative and emotional contact with parents and relatives, as well as with the environment in which children live and develop, the family nucleus should transmit the basics in the educational process of the developing infant.

The tasks assumed by parents will set the psycho-emotional development of their children, their self-esteem within the maturation process, and the tools that will psychologically define their potentialities (and also weaknesses) in the long road of life.

This **Parent's Guide** has an approach based on multisensory activities for the excellent development of the child. It is also focused on stimulating sports, art, music, singing, culture, dance, among other interests that favor the good formation of our children.

This guide is a simply written book that will oxygenate parents' brains and prepare their minds to overcome any obstacles in the future.

Let's keep in mind that: The development of the human being begins from the very moment of conception, that is why it must be evaluated from the prenatal level and go through a control during the whole childhood.

ORIGIN OF SELF-ESTEEM

Presently of conception, the union of the sperm and the egg in the mother's uterus; the load of messages that the child receives begins.

The developing child feels and suffers all that its mother experiences; first [energetically] through thoughts, feelings, emotions, and sensations that are manifestations of energy in the organism. Manifestations that are presented in the baby in gestation in the form of electrical and chemical (electrochemical) reactions that spread throughout the body, through an [intra-organic language]. And, that the baby; in formation, registers it in its subconscious mind, without having the opportunity to reject or accept it.

As a consequence of this unconscious act; the child who begins to grow in its mother's womb begins to perceive with clarity, but without linguistic comprehension, the impressions of what happens inside and outside the mother's womb.

This is how the child's SELF-ESTEEM begins to [originate]; since the child begins to perceive certain feelings and emotions through the mother and her environment. Environment that he now learns to recognize in [a psychological way] and that, in effect, this will form part of his unconscious register. These are the first [origins] of mental programming in children.

Understanding the Phases of Self-Esteem

FIRST PHASE: ABSORPTION.

When the birth of the child has already taken place; every external stimulus will influence the newborn and will create an emotional impression that will influence the process of its development through the years.

This **FIRST PHASE** is known as **ABSORPTION** and is the phase that goes from birth to approximately seven years of age.

At this stage, the child does not possess a fully developed cognitive capacity; for now, and will develop later. [*He is conscious, but he is not aware, that he is conscious*].

This period is called ABSORPTION because the infant reacts to the external stimuli of its environment and surrounding environment, *[As if it were a sponge, passively absorbing all the information presented to it]*.

This is the phase in which the child is most susceptible to learning, and in which he linguistically encodes in his subconscious the information he receives, whether good or bad, positive or negative.

Information and experiences that are being modeled and programmed by language in the infant's mind.

SECOND PHASE: MODELING.

This SECOND PHASE in the child's development is called MODELING and goes from the age of eight to approximately thirteen years old.

In this period of time; the child begins to question everything more intensely, begins to debate his ideas and question certain situations in his environment.

[They begin to become more aware of their consciousness]. They begin to select more conscientiously what should enter their mind and be linguistically encoded in their brain.

In this phase of MODELING, children begin to give more importance to what they witness and stop passively absorbing what they hear and what they see others do. In other words, they learn to evaluate situations and events for themselves before accepting them.

In the MODELING phase, 90% of the behavioral patterns, programming or mental maps, habits, and paradigms (criteria, judgments, and evaluation measures) have already been programmed and linguistically encoded in our children's minds.

THIRD PHASE: SOCIALIZATION.

This THIRD PHASE of child development is called SOCIALIZATION and runs from age fourteen to twenty-one.

In this period, adolescents want to become more independent, more self-sufficient, so they avoid spending too much time with their parents. Most young people prefer to spend more time with their peers and contemporary friends at the same age.

AT THIS CRUCIAL STAGE, IS WHERE ADOLESCENTS TRY TO ASSERT THEIR PERSONALITY; [although deep down many of them will continue to be like their parents].

"Theoretically, everything is completed at the age of twenty-one, I say [theoretically] because there are children over fifty who have not yet ["left"] their parents' homes. They may not live with them physically and geographically, [the father has already died, and the mother lives thousands of miles away]. However, emotionally and psychologically they are still or live [inside the home] because they have not yet developed their own personal independence."

In summary, we can say that our children's SELF-ESTEEM is ORIGINATED at the moment of gestation, and is FORMED in the years following birth. As the days go by, children will eventually learn to DEVELOP a healthy and balanced behavior according to what they perceive in their environment and surroundings.

Subsequently, the SELF-ESTEEM and DEVELOPMENT of our children is consolidated in adulthood and is manifested through marriage, home, families, child-rearing, social and professional relationships that more clearly show the behavior, personality, attitude, and character of each human being.

WE MUST PREPARE OURSELVES TO BE PARENTS

Parents, as we have learned so far, are the first teachers in the home. Therefore, it is essential and important to always maintain active communication links between the two.

From birth, the child must get used to being independent. There are basic points that must be fulfilled so that the personality of our children can develop in a self-sufficient way from the first months of life:

It is recommended that as the baby grows, he should not always sleep next to his parents. The infant should learn little by little to be alone in his crib, under the supervision and protection of his parents.

From the age of one year, we must teach our child to eat alone, and to do so, he/she must count on the example of the parents.

When bathing and grooming them, they should be taught the dynamics so that they begin to do it on their own, without neglecting them at any time.

When dressing and undressing our children, it is appropriate to give them the opportunity to also do it on their own so that they acquire practice and develop the habit. At this point, we must guide them with patience and applaud them *(reward them / congratulate them / recognize their effort)* when they achieve their goal. This step is crucial to motivate them to continue learning.

Another recommendation is to avoid kissing them on the lips. We can do it in special moments, only if the occasion requires it. Similarly, it is of vital importance, never kiss them in their intimate or erogenous zones, and only do it preferably on the cheeks or forehead, and accompany it with a hug. This will strengthen the bonds of love and union between the two.

Let's keep in mind that everything we try to teach our children, must be presented playfully, and at the same time, with a defined purpose. That is to say, with rules, to form habits that tend to ingrain values in children.

Applying these tasks between the ages of zero to seven *(absorption phase)* will be a continuous work in parents, a slow process, where children will be constantly observing, curious, inquiring and asking about everything.

At this stage, a process called neuronal myelination comes into play. In this process of the absorption phase, the central nervous system is in full growth, and therefore, children easily record (absorb) everything their senses pick up.

For this reason, it is necessary to dedicate effective and real time to know their desires, reactions, and moods.

It is also convenient to evaluate the intelligence process that is innate to them, and to offer them sincere support, motivating them, recognizing their achievements together with an affective-emotional relationship centered on love.

We must understand that children imitate everything they observe in their relationships with their parents. In this phase of absorption, at the age of seven, the child will have in his mind a "movie" recorded about what he learned from his parents. And his optimal state to reach his full psychological and emotional development will depend on what he learned in this first stage of his life.

Then comes the (modeling phase), which goes from eight to thirteen years of age. This is the appropriate stage to motivate them to practice a sport or encourage them to develop a taste for art, music, singing, participatory play and other healthy activities as an educational factor for the complete development of the child.

Let's keep in mind that: Every educational learning process has rules, schedules, orders, goals, motivation, creativity, etc.

ACTIVITIES TO RESTRUCTURE THE CHILD'S HEALTHY PERSONALITY

1. Waking up early and getting up alone, without parental help.

2. To have a few minutes previously agreed upon for personal grooming.

3. Dressing as if playing, respecting the previously established rules.

4. Breakfast with the family (Family sharing with parents and siblings).

5. Attend school with joy and true enthusiasm.

6. Eating food during lunch at the dining room table.

7. Do homework on their own, always counting on the supervision, guidance, and collaboration of their parents.

8. Take intermediate breaks as a distraction, for your personal enjoyment.

9. Dinner, likewise, should be with the family, all together, to strengthen the bonds of family unity before bedtime.

10. Go to bed at an early hour, according to their age. For parents, it is advisable to set aside time to read a story, sing a song, or simply share quality time and affection before bedtime.

WE ARE IN THE AGE OF TECHNOLOGY

Being in a stage of modernization and digital technology. We must keep in mind that today's children are much more familiar with virtual video games, social networks, viral videos, mobile applications, live broadcasting programs, among others.

Therefore, as responsible parents, we must teach our children to program themselves with adequate schedules, previously established, so that children can have enough time for the measured use of this type of technological and digital tools. Either for their study, training or for their enjoyment in their free time.

The important thing is to encourage our children to develop their own creativity through other more conventional means, such as: Reading children's texts, playful activities, outdoor games with other children. As well as motivating them to develop skills in dance, music, sports, art, among other activities of their interest.

Playing and sharing activities with other children of the same age are a significant factor not only for the healthy and balanced formation of the child's personality, but also for the self-discovery of his or her skills, competencies, and talents.

It is essential to emphasize that, in the initial school stage, children should be prepared with values and a good education that will govern their behavior in the classroom. This allows them to socialize with other children of their age, learning to share, respect other classmates, be obedient to the instructions of their teachers and above all maintain a balanced behavior.

It must be considered that, in most educational centers, only academic knowledge will be given to our children. In many other cases, they will be provided with extracurricular activities together with professional pedagogical advice.

However, it is necessary to educate the child from our homes, to guide our youth and adolescents in the warmth of the home. And thus, receive a comprehensive education, not only academic, but also a comprehensive training along with the accompaniment of their parents.

Similarly, it is advisable to motivate them to practice a sport in one of the various disciplines and specialties that exist. And, above all, it is of vital importance to encourage them to participate in sports activities with which the child, young person or adolescent feels more comfortable and identified.

Without neglecting chores or responsibilities at home in which their participation should be basic and essential, such as *(making the bed, washing their underwear, personal hygiene, cleaning their room, collaborating in small household chores, etc.).*

Likewise, their creativity, intelligence, curiosity, and skills should be enhanced while they are still babies, with didactic games, singing, dancing, and other interactive and technological options suitable for their happy and healthy upbringing.

MOTIVATE VS. IMPOSE

The importance of learning to encourage our children without imposing anything on them authoritatively.

As I said before, from the beginning of his school learning, the child must learn to socialize with the other classmates, and turn them into his first friends, as part of a process to improve his quality of communication based on brotherly and sisterly affection.

For this reason, parents should give importance to the quality time they spend and share with their children. Therefore, it is advisable to encourage our children by providing them with quality time and not only quantity in the hours they spend together.

Another good recommendation is to encourage our children to participate in extracurricular activities, such as sports, which allow children to achieve optimal physical and mental performance. Other activities that we could encourage in our children could be dance, music, singing, art, or any other activity that our children feel comfortable with.

It is important to emphasize at this point that excesses should be avoided. That is to say, it is one thing to encourage the child to participate in some of these activities with which he/she feels identified. It is quite another to force him to participate in activities in which he does not feel comfortable.

It is also essential to emphasize at this point that it is the child, young person or adolescent who must choose for themselves the activity they wish to do. As parents, we can guide them, but we should never authoritatively impose them to do what we want them to do, without their consent.

I repeat, as parents we can guide our children and motivate them to do some activity, without imposing, forcing, or demanding that our children do any activity that is not pleasurable for them. Remember, we are their parents, not their masters. And they have every right to select what they like to do, as long as it is positive for their physical, emotional, psychological and intellectual development.

THE IMPORTANCE OF PROPER EDUCATION FROM HOME

Parents should pay attention to the educational process of their children. The observation of the development of their multiple intelligences and talents is of vital importance for their integration in social, physical, recreational, academic, and competitive activities.

This will help children reach their maximum potential, and excellence in all the activities they do.

Parents should be fully convinced of their mission in the upbringing and education of their children, with the objective of contributing to their psycho-emotional well-being at every stage of their formation.

As a parent, I understand that sometimes we will find ourselves at home with situations that are difficult to cope with. Events that may be out of our hands.

Or, puzzling circumstances in which we will not know how to respond or act to resolve those latent family conflicts.

Ideally, we should learn to resolve these issues with patience, wisdom, and correctness within the rules of respect, calm, prudence, and affection towards all the members of our family.

Let us keep in mind that as our children grow older, they will begin to show different behaviors and attitudes related to the physical, cognitive, emotional and psychological changes they experience due to their age and development at different stages.

Therefore, as parents, we must be prepared for these puberty changes. And remember that we ourselves as adults were once impulsive children, teenagers, and adolescents.

For this reason, it is crucial to integrate guidelines for timely and correct disciplinary decisions and actions. To prevent or correct incidents that may occur, in the most effective and loving manner possible.

To achieve this goal, it is advisable to seek to strengthen the bonds at home with all the members who make up our family. At the same time, that we instill good habits in our children from an early age. Habits such as respect, good communication, understanding, trust, integrity, and discipline. Habits that will allow our children to be better people, built on good principles and values, as they grow up.

HOW TO AVOID EGOCENTRISM

We speak of egocentrism in children to refer to the selfish attitude and behavior of those children who feel that the world revolves around them, their needs, desires, and whims. It refers to that indifferent attitude that children develop towards others, which does not allow the child to put aside his or her pride to make room for someone else's needs.

To avoid this attitude in our children, the child must be formed from an early age, with the habit of thinking and reflecting on their actions. We must teach children to develop empathy for others, we must instill in them respect for other people and for themselves.

Through this conscious practice, the child will achieve a social, psychological and emotional balance, which allows him/her to learn to socialize with other people in an adequate manner.

In addition to acquiring the ability to develop a healthy self-esteem and a good self-concept, self-image and positive self-perception of others.

MULTIPLE INTELLIGENCES

Imagination, creativity, art, music, singing, dance, outdoor activities, group recreational games and sports are all part of a formative process that is consistent with the innate abilities with which our children were born.

These activities can strengthen each of the types of multiple intelligences that exist, and which all human beings have to a lesser or greater extent.

Multiple Intelligences According to Howard Gardner

According to **Howard Gardner,** there are eight predominant intelligences. Each of them is characterized by specific skills and abilities. Later on, emotional intelligence was incorporated, promoted by **Daniel Goleman**, becoming the 9th intelligence.

1. ***Linguistic Intelligence.*** *It is the ability to use language in all its expressions and manifestations.*
2. ***Musical Intelligence.*** *It is the ability to perceive and express oneself through musical forms.*
3. ***Logical-mathematical intelligence.*** *It is the ability to solve mathematical calculations and put into practice logical reasoning.*
4. ***Kinesthetic Body Intelligence.*** *It is the ability to express ideas and feelings through the expression of the human body.*
5. ***Spatial Intelligence.*** *It is the ability to perceive the visual and spatial environment, transforming, understanding, and comprehending it.*
6. ***Intrapersonal Intelligence.*** *It is the ability to develop profound knowledge of oneself.*
7. ***Interpersonal Intelligence.*** *It is the ability to relate to others, developing empathy and social interaction.*
8. ***Naturalistic Intelligence.*** *It is the ability to observe and study the*

elements that make up nature (objects, animals, and plants).

9. ***Emotional Intelligence.*** *This concept helps to connect with other people, build relationships, communicate more effectively, resolve conflicts and above all learn to express our feelings.*

STIMULATE THE DEVELOPMENT OF SKILLS

As we mentioned earlier, imagination, creativity, art, music, dance, outdoor activities, recreational games, as well as sports, among others. These are ideal ways to stimulate the healthy development and integral skills of our children.

These activities strengthen each of the multiple intelligences that children have to a lesser or greater degree.

Playful learning methods are significant for the formation and development of our children through practical experiences that allow them to maximize the best of their abilities.

Therefore, it is highly recommended to encourage the practice of sports, art, music, communication and social participation as a process of formation and optimal development in the achievement of children's integral performance.

Likewise, it is imperative to create in the family nucleus, the need to apply the didactic - ludic game as a determining factor in the education of our children.

JAPANESE CULTURE AND PHILOSOPHY IN EDUCATION

We are aware that changing family and cultural education in our country is difficult. However, as parents, we must be willing to contribute and complement our children with adequate functions to form a healthy and balanced child, youth and adolescent, who has the right tools to defend themselves against the adversities of daily life.

I will tell you about Japanese culture and its philosophy in education, a way of life and teaching that I found interesting.

In Japan, children are not tested until the fourth grade of elementary school. Before that, the priority is for them to learn more about life.

For example, one of their first teachings is good manners. In their early formative years, they are brought up in an upbringing that instills respect for others and for animals. They are also taught to seek the truth and to care for nature.

One of the cultural factors that make Japanese schools stand out is that they do not hire cleaners. It is the children themselves who clean everything, and they do it in shifts. As a civic duty in favor of all present.

In this way, from an early age, they learn to work as a team and to help each other. They learn to value the work of others and their own, and at the same time, they learn to be more respectful of the environment and their fellow human beings.

Japanese children are prepared nutritious food and eat in community, thus creating more friendly and cordial relationships.

Discipline, on the other hand, is the art of the Japanese school, punctuality is basic and essential in all aspects.

As we have learned from Japanese culture and its philosophy, there are so many good things to learn, my dear parents, that today I invite you to reflect on these teachings.

CHILDREN IN THEIR BODY, FEELINGS, AND EMOTIONS

As a parent, we must avoid forcing our children to submit to involuntary emotional affection or unwanted physical contact just to avoid offending a family member or hurting a person's feelings.

This is because forcing a child to give a kiss or a hug when they do not wish to do so is an imposition, which over time can make the youngest members of the household vulnerable to pedophiles.

Sisterly affection should never be imposed. Vinka Jackson, author of the children's book: "MY BODY IS A GIFT". She comments that: It is not recommended that adults force children, youth, and adolescents into physical and affective-emotional relationships without their consent.

Our children should have the right to choose whom to love, cherish, fraternize, hug, share, and kiss. As parents, our duty is to teach them ethical values and moral principles that allow children, youth, and adolescents to learn to socialize in a healthy and balanced way. Focused on respect and empathy towards others. Without authoritarian imposition by their parents or authority figures.

The message they receive is that they have the right to freedom of choice, that they are respected as individuals and are allowed to show physical or emotional affection only to those they care about.

It has been shown that imposing (forcing) our children to give physical or emotional affection to unrequited people; just to look good, to appear in front of others or simply by parental whim. Eventually, it creates children, youth, and adolescents more likely to be victims of bullying and adults vulnerable to sleeping with someone just to please or to keep the other person happy.

For this reason, let's respect our children and the decisions they make about their bodies, emotions, and feelings. Our children are independent people, so we should never impose (force) them to do something they don't really want to do.

An example: A family relative comes home to visit. ***How would you react?***

A) Tell the child: "***give your uncle a kiss and a hug.***"
B) Saying to the child: ***"Say hello to your uncle".***

Answer honestly, do *you let your child greet with a kiss and hug only when he feels like it, or do you force and impose it on him?*

CHILDREN ARE A REFLECTION OF THEIR PARENTS

"**Daddy, Never Forget About Me**" Never forget that you are my hero, and that because I admire you so much, I am always watching everything you do.

Remember that your example will mark the person I will be in the future. If I see that you are a hardworking father and lovingly provide for our family. I will never sit back and wait for things to fall from the sky, but like you, I will be a good provider.

If I see that you love mom, you respect her, you treat her well, you communicate, you are there when she needs you, and you support her in everything in your power. I will be a man who will know how to treat women well.

If I see that you are honest, upright, live righteously; avoiding lying, manipulating or taking advantage of others in any way. I will be an honest man who lives a life centered on principles and values.

If you are a man of good, who helps others and serves your fellow man. You will make me feel happy at all times to be your son and follow your example.

If I see that you take care of my grandparents with love, dedication and patience, I will never leave you forgotten when you are old, but I will gladly take care of you every day of my life".

Dad, never forget that love can never be bought with gifts. I don't need toys; I need quality time with you and your company. Keep in mind that my greatest gift is the moments we share together, which will become pleasant memories and experiences.

Daddy, I just wish that for a moment, you would turn off the TV even though you are watching one of your favorite movies and avoid using your cell phone and leave everything else aside, when I tell you that I need to talk to you.

If I ask you to talk to me, it is because I trust you, and I need to hear from your wise words, to overcome something I may be going through.

Daddy, I have to feel your support in difficult times, to feel you by my side when I get sick or when I have a challenging day at school.

Dad, never forget that you make me happy just to see that you love me and that you are proud that I am your son.

Dad, I love it when you carry me on your shoulders, and hug me when I get home, your presence gives me security.

Dad, I really appreciate it when you teach me new things. And I know I can count on you anytime I need you.

Daddy, I love it when you hug Mommy and tell her you love her. You spend time with her and help her with chores and household responsibilities.

"Dad, never forget that you are a source of inspiration to me. And my admiration for you is so great that my little eyes light up when I see you coming home and giving affection to all of us in the family. Therefore, I ask that you never damage this special image I have of you. Finally, I only ask that you always stay by my mommy's and my side, and remember that I am learning from you".

HOW CHILDREN LEARN

Humans perceive and learn in different ways and through different sensory channels *(sight, hearing, touch, taste, and smell).*

Nowadays, there are many educational processes to raise our children in a more efficient way. Today, there are many psychotherapeutic and alternative methods that we can follow.

For example, the life coach or life coaching specialized in parenting, family psychotherapy specialized in strengthening the family nucleus, NLP, or neurolinguistic programming as an alternative methodology to help in the programming of new behavioral habits.

Whatever we choose, the most important thing is to consider the needs of our children, and the purpose for which we have decided to go to a specialist.

However, as parents, we also have the empirical tools and experience to guide our children to receive a healthy and balanced education.

At times, it will be vital to inform ourselves, to learn new parenting methods and to have to unlearn old patterns if necessary. The fundamental thing is to have the desire to give the best education to our children; even if that requires us to learn how to do it.

As I started in this section, at the beginning of this point. I commented that all human beings, including children and adults, learn in different ways and through different sensory channels. *"**Visual** what we see, **Auditory what** we hear, **Kinesthetic** what we touch and feel, "**Olfactory** what we smell and **Gustatory what** we taste or taste."*

Through these multisensory sensations, we come into contact with the world, which allows us to learn and receive information from the outside, whether we are aware of it or not.

That is, the 5 senses *(sight, hearing, touch, taste, and smell)* are the means by which we process our thoughts, feelings and emotions, making sense of the information we receive, and act accordingly.

As we have learned so far, human beings use our 5 senses to learn. In particular, we most frequently use the *visual, auditory and kinesthetic* channels to explore and delimit the outside world.

However, we can only perceive a small portion of it. That small part is then filtered by our experiences, culture, beliefs, principles, values, interests, etc.

For this reason, it is important to emphasize that each human being, according to his childhood formation, the environment where he grew up and the influences he received in his surroundings, refines to a certain degree one representational system more than another.

Either *"the **Visual** is what we see, the **Auditory** is what we hear or the **Kinesthetic** is what we touch and feel"*. Although in one way or another, all people including children and adults can develop all 3 sensory channels at the same time to a greater or lesser degree.

With this in mind, as parents we can begin to teach our children in a didactic way using the 3 sensory channels most used in learning, which are: The **visual sense** *(the child learns what he sees)* the **auditory sense** *(the child learns from what he hears)* and finally, the **kinesthetic sensory sense** (*children learn with movements, sensations, emotions, etc.)*.

Below, I will share some tips and recommendations to apply them in the education and training of our children from the comfort of home, without the need for the accompaniment of a professional.

5 WAYS TO HELP CHILDREN LEARN AT HOME

How do children learn?

By Exploration: Touching, knocking, using contact *(**kinesthetic**)*.

By Experimentation: Tasting, smelling, learning by cause and effect or trial and error *(**gustatory**, **olfactory**, and **sensory**)*.

By Repetition: Doing things over and over again *(in psychology, this process is known as **neural anchoring**)*.

By Imitation: Copying all those around them, whether adults or other children *(in psychology, it is called **modeling**)*.

By Their 5 senses: They learn through what they see *(**sight**), what they* hear *(**hearing**), what* they touch *(**touch**), what they* smell *(**smell**)* and what they taste *(**taste**)*.

In conclusion: Children learn from and from everything in their immediate environment. ***And what is around a child?*** A great variety of things, people and very diverse situations, that is, an infinity of **multisensory stimuli**.

However, it is the adult who is responsible for mediating, transferring and translating each of these stimuli for the healthy education and formation of the child.

The mediating role of parents in the learning process

The parents' role is to facilitate the child's understanding of his or her environment, to help them make a bond that is suitable for the child.

Today, there is increasing evidence and research demonstrating the impacts on child development through positive and responsive interactions with parents, creating more psychologically and emotionally balanced children.

On the other hand, it has been demonstrated that when teachers manage behavioral aspects in an intentional manner, attend to the child's interests and channel their attention in a receptive way; children improve their behavior in the classroom and also have better academic performance, thus developing a better interaction with their classmates.

The siblings, the caregiver, the other children in the child care center, classmates, or school teachers are necessary and contribute to the process of formation and learning of our children. However, they are not enough; they are only part of the process.

Child development is enhanced in a more balanced way with parental interaction primarily in the home. Next comes the preschool, where children begin to interact with others their age. This is followed by school, where many children spend a considerable proportion of their time.

However, while each of them will provide our children with experiences or academic education that are essential. Again, they are not everything.

The presence of parents at home together with family sharing is and will always be what provides security to children and reinforces their self-esteem.

Here are 5 ways parents can enhance children's learning at home:

1. Pay attention to the non-verbal signals that the child transmits, and follow his or her interests. Beyond offering affection and affection, which are fundamental for the good psycho-emotional development of our children. The adult can learn to identify and respond to the forms of communication or non-verbal language of the child, for example:

A) – Naming the object or action of interest: If the child points to an object, without uttering any words. The ideal would be to ask, ***"What are you pointing to?*** Ah! We identify the object and reaffirm ***"The storybook of the sun and the moon"***. And then, when the child responds affirmatively, we hand him/her the storybook. This allows the child to learn to communicate and also stimulates him to express in words what he wants.

B) – Responding if the baby babbles or the child smiles when performing an action together: At that time we can ask ***"You like it when I tickle your feet, don't you?"*** *or* ***"You like it when we spend some time together, don't you?"***. These actions will reaffirm the parent-child relationship. And it will allow the child to feel that he is being appreciated and that his parents are attentive to his needs.

C) – Talk about what is happening: When we are dressing the child, we can say ***"Yes! I'm putting on your socks, so you won't get cold feet"***. Soon you will be able to do it by yourself, since you are smart, and you learn very fast;

meanwhile I will be here to support you while you learn. This phrase allows the child to see that we understand his needs, while at the same time stimulating him to feel the desire to start doing it himself.

Introduce new concepts, naming everything in the environment. During bath time, for example, elaborate on how hot or cold the water is, how dry or wet the floor is, the parts of the child's body, mentioning and pointing them out one by one. Or, at lunchtime, take advantage of mealtime to talk about the textures, sizes, shapes, and colors of food.

All these interactions will allow the child to learn to differentiate between things in his environment, to be aware of his surroundings and to learn from everything around him.

3. Expand the child's knowledge. When watching a movie or reading a story together, if the child says: "***woof-woof***", "***meow***" or "***moo***", add: "***yes, it's a big dog, and it has four legs!***" pointing to them. "***Bravo, yes, it is a small kitten, and it is very hairy***", "***Son how clever you are, yes, it is a cow, and it is white with black spots***"! These actions will let the child know that we are attentive and above all we stimulate him to learn to name things correctly and to differentiate the changes that exist between them.

4. Play! Playing is the primary means of learning for the child, as well as great fun. By playing, parents can participate and encourage role-playing together with their children, whether they are toddlers or teenagers, **remember that children and young people imitate everything adults do!** If we are a good example for them and spend quality time together, they will learn to become more sociable and spontaneous.

In addition, introduce challenges and problems that the child has to solve: for example, playing to open a jar and take out what is inside, to assemble a puzzle, to find an object that we have hidden, to teach him to learn a new sport, to motivate him to do something artistic or creative, and a long etcetera. Everything will depend on the age of the child, the talents, and abilities he/she possesses and above all on his/her tastes, preferences, and needs.

Recommendation: Parents can vary the game, posing increasingly complex challenges, always keeping it achievable for them according to their age and abilities. If a game is simple, and the child can solve it immediately, he gets bored and loses interest. However, if it is too complex, the child will get frustrated and stop trying. For this reason, it is important to go up a level, little by little, always keeping the new challenges somewhat more difficult than the previous one, but always keeping it achievable for the child or adolescent. Another recommendation, recognize their efforts, sincerely praise their triumphs and support them when things get difficult for them. Show them that you are there to teach them with love. And turn that opportunity into a beautiful memory for both of you.

5. Recognize and reinforce attempts and achievements positively: As I mentioned earlier, congratulating the child with applause, kisses, hugs, or a special detail are great ways to encourage them to always do their best. Other ways would be verbalizing their achievement and attempts, praising them with sincere words when they give their best effort and acknowledging them with words of encouragement will promote their self-esteem and encourage them to keep learning, trying and enjoying it.

Benefits of Parent-Child Interaction

All of these practices help the child in multiple ways:

1. Develop their language. Talking to our children regularly, reading them stories and singing. They expose and familiarize them with many new words, which they will understand and internalize, and that little by little, later on, they will introduce in their vocabulary.

2. Promote their cognitive and motor skills. The child becomes familiar with complex concepts such as cause and effect, trial and error. Likewise, he learns to perceive the difference, boy or girl, light or dark, cold or heat. In addition, the child learns to develop analytical, rational thinking in simple situations, such as: The permanence of objects *(the object does not disappear just because you no longer see it)* or *(things do not change just because they say or think so)*.

3. Develop and stimulate aspects of executive function. Such as, for example, attention, perseverance, self-regulation, among others, through facing and overcoming new challenges.

4. Encouraging their creativity and socioemotional development. Promoting affection, love and sympathy, the affectionate and respectful bond between children and their parents. All these actions promote a warm and close relationship between both.

5. Provoking their curiosity and encouraging them to want to learn new things. Incentivizing them to develop new skills, potentiating their already latent talents, helping them to recognize their capabilities and limitations.

In conclusion: It is important for the learning and formation of the child to exercise the memory, stimulate thinking, work on attention to things and people with a learning process that takes advantage of the multiple multisensory capabilities that our children have.

FACT: Lack of time, fatigue, the presence of other children and sometimes other responsibilities often limit the quantity and quality of interactions between parents and their children.

Therefore, as responsible parents, it is crucial that we remember all the benefits they bring to their children when they take the quality time to share with them and be present in their formation and education from home.

All adults, from our sphere as parents, relatives, neighbors, caregivers, teachers, have the responsibility to play this valuable mediating role in our relationship and interaction with children, thus contributing to promote their development to their maximum potential.

WHAT HAPPENS WHEN YOU YELL AT YOUR CHILDREN?

As we have learned so far, raising our children is a beautiful process. However, it can also be stressful at times. It requires a lot of emotional control and training to avoid losing control in situations that may upset or worry us at times.

When yelling becomes habitual in the family, even if we apologize later, there will be no turning back, since it leaves emotional traces.

Constant yelling has a negative impact on the brain and neurological development of children. According to recent studies conducted at the University of Michigan, led by psychologist Piedad Gonzalez. When we scream, the following happens:

1-. The act of screaming in an evolutionary way has the function of alerting of some eminent danger. When we yell at our children, regardless of age or the reason for the event, stress hormones ***(cortisol*** *and* ***adrenaline)*** are triggered in them, predisposing the body to flee or attack. Producing two proven reactions.

a) The child becomes tense, and his thoughts are blocked.

b) The child goes into attack mode and rebels.

2. When we yell at children, the corpus callosum of the brain, which is located between the ***two hemispheres,*** receives the blood flow, which affects their emotional balance and attention span.

Children who have been subjected to this type of verbal violence, in the vast majority, develop behavioral problems that cause low cognitive performance. In addition, it encourages fights and conflicts with other children, prompting them to tell lies to their parents and, in many other cases, the opposite happens, leading to the appearance of symptoms such as depression, sadness and social isolation.

Shouting impacts the child's self-esteem. The child will feel that he/she is not appreciated or loved. Although this is not the intention of their parents. So, *why do we do it*, why do we *yell at our children, why do we let our stress get the better of us, why do we explode and pour all our anger on them*, why *do we repeat the patterns of upbringing we had in our childhood and use them against our family?*

To have a more functional family and give a better upbringing, education, and training to our children. We must be willing to unlearn those habits and behaviors.

Controlling our temper, developing a balanced emotional intelligence, and cultivating patience is healthy so that our children never get involved in this cycle of verbal violence.

DISCIPLINING OUR CHILDREN WITHOUT YELLING AND SCREAMING IS POSSIBLE

Learning to live together in harmony in a world where violence reigns is an arduous task because a conflicting society naturally influences us.

However, all parents require the effort, perseverance, collaboration, and commitment of both spouses to reorient the process of education and formation of their children in a balanced way, based on the pillars of ethical values and moral principles.

Since, these fundamentals will be internalized in our children as they grow up. Forging in them a healthy personality, creating a better future perspective with higher standards of living. And as a result, a more cordial and pleasant social life.

It is a challenge to learn to recognize our weaknesses as parents, and to assume the responsibility to begin to correct them in a timely manner.

Similarly, it is a challenge to learn to live together with our children, without using verbal or physical violence.

However, learning to be better parents every day, learning to live a balanced life, psychologically and emotionally, will result in a better coexistence with our children. In addition, learning to develop emotional intelligence allows us to better control and express our feelings towards them.

This will lead to a reduction of conflicts in the home, leaving aside shouting and any other type of verbal aggression. Thus improving communication between parents and children and encouraging family unity and trust towards all members of the family.

HOW TO TEACH, EDUCATE AND RAISE OUR CHILDREN FROM A RESPECTFUL POINT OF VIEW

We transmit firmness and kindness to our children when we respect their needs and look after them.

A couple of years ago, I was with my youngest daughter on my way to a girls' clothing store. Walking into the store with her hand in hand, we witnessed a rather upset and stressed out father slap his about 3-year-old daughter across the face.

I'm not going to recreate the scene because you can imagine how the little girl's face looked, not to mention the heartbreaking cry and her panic-stricken face looking at her two parents without understanding anything.

Nor will I go into detail on the momentary pain and suffering that the girl was going through at that moment. What I will do, however, is to tell what happened immediately afterward around us, which is what caught my attention the most.

On the one hand, my daughter squeezed my hand, frightened, and then immediately asked me:

"Dad, isn't there anything ***so bad in the world that little girl has done that her father would beat her like that?"*** (Silence)...

At the same time, I began to hear the murmurs of the adults who were near the scene, as they said to their children: **some in favor of what happened, while others were strongly against the act.**

"What could he have done to get beaten!".

"Even if he had it coming, the father shouldn't have acted like that!".

"See what happens when children don't obey?".

"So he won't do what he did again!"

"A good slap in the face in time, and the nonsense goes away!"

"I don't agree with a parent treating their child that way."

"For God's sake, somebody does something, please!".

It is true that my daughter and I remained silent from the impact for a few seconds. Then, I approached little by little to mediate and as I did, other parents also tried to do so.

However, millions of times I prefer to keep silent in a situation like this, before answering some lies and nonsense opinions you just read. *Each answer, tells us a lot about the adult who uttered it, and the type of parent he/she is, in that given situation.*

Do we really believe we have the right to treat our children with such disrespect? Do you, as an adult, not make mistakes and still want to be treated with dignity? Do you think your child learns anything from being mistreated in this way?

Every time a parent acts in this way (and I'm not talking about a slap necessarily included), they do it supposedly for love. That is because they want the best for their children, they do whatever it takes for them to learn. Or so they think.

However, you know that in this way the message of love NEVER gets through and on the contrary leaves deep wounds in your children. Physical or verbal abuse was never, and will never be, the way to correct your children.

Let him reflect with you on the right way, in which love does come, and the right way to discipline your children with respect:

How does the message of love from parents to children get through?

Mom, Dad, your message of love comes to me when I make mistakes and help me understand what I have done wrong, and how I can learn to do better next time, instead of resorting to punishment.

Remember that I am a little person who is investigating the world, and learning little by little. Or don*'t you remember that years ago you were also a boy or a girl and did the same thing?*

Mom, Dad, your message of love reaches me when you validate my emotions and teach me to recognize my feelings, but not my behavior when I am wrong. Please, when I am angry, never say to me: *"Don't be angry, daughter, you look like mommy"*, or when I am sad, never say things like, *"Don't cry, it's not worth it, besides, children don't cry"*! Those comments affect me more than they can help.

The only thing I need is that you accompany me to understand my emotion, that you put yourself in my place and see the world through my little eyes because only in this way, you will teach me to better understand and manage my emotions and understand my feelings in the right way.

Mom, Dad, your message of love reaches me when you set limits with kindness, love, and firmness at the same time, when you teach me what is right and what is wrong, how far I can go and where I should stop, and you teach me all these things with respect.

Because remember that you must respect yourself so that I can learn from you. You must be my example and my role model.

Comments: This incident that I have told you about at the beginning is a sample of millions of similar situations that happen in the world day after day, and that as parents we must prevent them from happening again.

"Whose crazy idea is it to believe that to make children behave well, you must first make them feel bad?" There is nothing falser than this statement. For that reason, I will teach you the right ways to **TEACH, EDUCATE AND RAISE OUR CHILDREN FROM RESPECT.**

Mutual respect between parents and children.

As parents, you teach firmness when you respect yourself and have emotional self-control in any situation; furthermore, you teach kindness and love when you respect the needs of your family environment and your children's own dignity.

In the initial example, it is clear that there is no respect or consideration for the little girl in the clothing store. However, please, never fall into the error of thinking that only when we resort to physical violence it is disrespectful to the little ones.

Or is it that *"the looks that kill"*, *"the ignorance or law of ice"*, *"the shouts or reproaches"*, *"see, I told you so! You are good for nothing"*? And countless other expressions that you use every day with your children***, aren't they just as humiliating and hurtful as the slap in the face?***

Furthermore, *who gave us permission to disrespect our children in this way, what do we assume children learn when we refer to them in this way, why don't you dare speak to your boss, a friend with whom you have differences, etc., and yet you do it to your child?* Is that fair enough? Doesn't that make you a cowardly bully in front of the little ones?

It gives us food for thought, doesn't it? Maybe it's because society is used to educating children this way, or because it's the way our parents have done it with us, or because we simply don't know how to do it any other way.

I don't know about you, but for me, these excuses are no longer valid. When you enter the world of Positive Discipline, you realize that there is a beautiful path that makes us better parents, and allows us to discipline our children with love and respect. Instead of reprimanding them inappropriately, bringing as consequences of those acts emotional wounds in the children.

Become aware of what I am telling you, and I guarantee that your thoughts, emotions and, consequently, your actions, will be aimed at respecting your child above all else.

And that doesn't mean that everything you do always turns out well, of course not. However, at least you sow good things to make it happen, and believe me, little by little, you yourself, your children, and your environment, will incorporate it. And the love, affection and respect between parents and children will grow.

What happens when we don't respect children? No matter how much we "scold out of love" and so that your children learn, I am sorry to tell you that, in this way, they will never learn anything productive.

The thoughts and feelings that children experience with such acts are much closer than you think to things like rebellion, resentment, revenge, or even withdrawal (submission).

Children feel inferior simply because they live in an adult world. And even if it is true that in many occasions their behaviors are not the most appropriate, this does not give us the right to humiliate them, reprimand them and make them feel guilty constantly.

If you want your children to respect you, you must start by respecting them first. Yes, this is so. Because our children learn by imitation, and they do it through mirror neurons.

No matter how much you tell them loudly to respect you, if after two minutes you are growling at them, you can be sure that they will keep this image engraved in their minds, and that, of course, sometime later they will reproduce these actions themselves because they have seen it repeatedly in their parents.

It is as if we are giving them permission to behave in this way with themselves, with us and with others. Since they learned that behavior from you. So, you should know that as parents, it is your responsibility to take care of how you share yourself in front of your children.

It is just as important to show respect to your child as it is to show respect to yourself. Remember, you are their role model. When you do things that you know will hurt your child, you are probably hurting yourself as well.

In addition, when you respect yourself, you are educating with firmness, and your child who learns the limits, essential for their healthy development.

Understanding the real motive behind the behavior.

When our children engage in bad behaviors according to adults, you must go beyond the behavior itself, which is all parents see.

So, you will need to learn to dive beneath the iceberg, that is, to understand what may be motivating the child to do what he or she is doing.

Without going into detail, one way to understand these behaviors and behaviors is to go into the emotion or emotions that the children are feeling at that precise moment.

Talking about what the child is feeling at each moment of the situation is crucial so that we can help our children to channel the behavior in the right direction and reach a solution if necessary.

When we help our children to do this, we will be promoting their emotional intelligence.

Once we manage to treat our child with respect, love, and discipline at the same time, we will be creating a safe environment for the child, which will encourage him/her to behave better, simply because he/she feels better, loved, and understood.

Effective communication.

To recapitulate, everything we have talked about so far must be put into practice with good communication and excellent aptitude. Because if there is one thing that distinguishes us from other animals, it is none other than language.

Language in communication generates realities, and to the extent that we use the right and respectful words with our children at the right time, a multitude of opportunities will open up that we can take advantage of to educate and teach our children in a firm and more respectful way at the same time.

"How many times have you repeated this phrase or heard it in your environment? One of the keys to getting your child to listen to you, is for you to listen to him too.

And silently reflect on this! *How often do you ask your children how they are feeling, what they need, or what are they thinking about?*

There is no better way to teach children to listen than by listening to them first.

Listen with your heart, without judgment, to understand, and then accompany your child to solve that challenge. *It's quite a challenge, isn't it?*

When we listen empathetically to our child, we will be able to invite them to reflect for themselves, and to say what they want to say. Instead of telling them what they have to say or what we think they have to say.

For this reason, we must learn as parents to listen to our children and allow them to express their opinions, openly express their concerns and sincerely communicate their emotions... ***Why do you ask yourself?***

Because then we will demand that they make decisions for themselves. And believe me, that will be difficult to do if our children have not first experienced what it means to have their judgment.

Educating with mutual respect implies educating with firmness and kindness at the same time.

So, I encourage you to think twice before you act, and think twice about what you are going to say to your child before reprimanding him/her. If you assume that the message or attitude on your part is not respectful, then don't do it, calm down first, take a deep breath, calm down, take control again, and then you can have a better result than letting yourself be carried away by the impulses of the moment.

So, I encourage you to think about what you want to teach your child in the future before you speak to him or her because only in this way will you use the right words in the most respectful way that your child needs to grow as a person.

Remember that your children will only learn when they feel safe by your side, when you validate their emotions, even if not their behaviors, and when they feel they can trust you, and that their mistakes are learning opportunities, and they are not penalized for them, but that together we all look for solutions. I assure you that your relationship will improve, your children will respect you, and the harmony in the family nucleus will be strengthened.

And you, ***what are you going to do differently to ensure that your message of love reaches your children?***

HOW TO EDUCATE OUR CHILDREN IN MODERN TIMES

These troubled times, such as the ones we live in today, are worrying about the protection of children's integrity. It is an unsafe world, where the nuclear family has become increasingly vulnerable, and the education of our children has been affected by a variety of social, cultural, and stereotypical influences.

The information age, digital technologies, social networks and different live broadcasting channels are now the main means of communication. Let us remember that children learn from what they observe and what they hear. Our children learn from repetition, they imitate everything they come into contact with regularly.

With this in mind, our responsibility as parents is to dedicate time to our children, to teach them what is best for them, allowing them to adapt to the modern processes of innovative education, without impacting the other areas of their lives.

For this reason, as parents we must be aware that the information age, digital technology, social networks, among others, is a reality. It is a reality, so assuming that our children are free from this influence is not real. The truth is that today's children are smarter and adapt quickly to these modern changes.

So, what can we do? The best thing to do is to allow our children to enjoy these new digital technologies and make the most of this interconnected world.

Of course, placing certain rules, established schedules, previous agreements of what they can or cannot do at certain times. In short, what I am trying to say is that as parents, we should take advantage of these new models of innovative education in favor of our children and not against it.

And how can we do this? As I mentioned before, by setting rules, schedules, previous agreements. For example, the child can use the tablet to play, as long as he has finished all his homework. Or, the youngster can watch his favorite series on a continuous broadcast, in his free time on weekends.

Another example could be: At mealtime, the whole family shares at the dining table without the distractions of cell phones and dedicate those brief periods of time to share and strengthen the family unit.

And like these, there are many other examples we could mention. What is relevant here, and what I want to emphasize, is that parents should seek to adopt the best measures that suit their particular needs. Since every family is different and every homeschooling process is different.

The question is, ***where are the parents' duty and the children's right?*** If we give a good example of attitude to our children, we set the rules within the home to strengthen family relationships through respect, discipline, and commitment. It will be much easier to form good children, obedient, honest and willing to comply with previously established agreements.

HOW TO ADAPT TO CHANGE AND TEACH OUR CHILDREN IN THE RIGHT WAY

The presence of fathers in the family nucleus is decreasing, so much so that sometimes fathers have less and less time to spend with their children.

The long working hours absent them from their children, to the point of not being able to give them the due attention they deserve. The consequences are absent, distant, dysfunctional families and, in the worst cases, marriages with so much responsibility that the upbringing of their children is left in the background.

Let us be aware that we must protect, help to raise our children with a lot of love, patience and discipline, directing their actions and goals in line with norms, rules, and values. And in this way, set in them a positive and consistent personal attitude, structured on the fullness of their potential, abilities, and talents. It is not easy I know, "I have never said it is easy. However, I promise you that it will not be impossible either... You just have to be willing to do your best, and you will see the positive results of your actions and good parenting for the rest of your life".

Children And Their Responsibilities

Children should learn to fulfill their obligations from an early age, to assume them responsibly without excuses, in a cordial manner and with a good disposition. If we teach our children to develop these habits since childhood, it is more likely that doing their homework will be easier, since they will see it as part of their routine.

Many parents have a hard time getting their children to obey them when they ask them to do their homework, get up early for school, do their homework, pick up their toys or help with household chores at home.

And in most of these cases, the reason is not disobedience, rebellion, or age. It is simply that, if we do not teach them from an early age to do their homework, we do not teach them to be responsible from an early age, and we never assign them small household chores.

Such as cleaning their room after playing, picking up their plate from the table and taking it to the sink after eating, getting up early every day as a matter of course, doing their homework as part of their schoolwork.

It is impossible to expect them to learn to be responsible overnight. Since children learn and forge their character from the first years of their childhood. So, it is our responsibility as parents to teach them from an early age, so that as they grow up, they internalize their responsibilities as something natural.

When children, from an early age, are left to fail to comply with their chores, duties, and responsibilities. It is very likely that they are being conditioned to a wrong education and bad behavior that will mark their way of being and acting in the future.

Therefore, discipline must be the most relevant when it comes to the upbringing of children at an early formative age. The first step, even more important than school education, is to forge a balanced and positive way of being so that they can face the future in a more responsible way.

RULES FOR RAISING OUR CHILDREN WELL.

1. **Assign simple tasks.** According to their age, constantly stimulate them to do small tasks. It is necessary to create habits, such as washing hands, brushing teeth, making the bed, picking up toys, putting dirty clothes in their place, preparing clothes for the next day, doing school homework, picking up his plate after eating, keeping his room tidy, participating in family decisions (having the child's opinion in simple situations).

The importance of creating routines. A daily schedule is ideal since it allows our child to be more disciplined when it comes to doing something. It is not enough for the child to make the bed only on weekends. He/she must get used to do the same task, at the same time, every day after getting up, that way he/she will learn to create routines.

The activities that our child will have to do every day will be internalized and will be engraved in him as habits. This will allow him to see them as part of his daily routine, and they will not be difficult for him later on as he grows up because he will be able to do them naturally.

3. Teach through consistency. The idea of daily routines will take hold in the child's mind. For repetition is the mother of all teaching. When a child from an early age is positively encouraged to do small tasks, with time and repetition, those routines will become habitual activities for him.

Recognize small accomplishments. It is important for children to realize that they are doing things right and that, by the way, their actions please their parents when they accomplish assigned tasks.

It is not necessary to always give them a reward because then they will then seek to do things, not out of their own free will, but to receive a reward.

Parents can show their appreciation and approval for what their children do through sincere verbal praise with phrases such as "Thank you, you did very well. I congratulate you.

Avoid negative phrases or statements. This type of statement affects children's behavior and cause them to become demotivated. Avoid statements such as "you're good for nothing," "you don't do anything right", "you're a fool", "you're useless".

With these words, as time goes by, children are marked for life and, as youngsters and adolescents, they will think that they cannot do certain things well, which will influence the development of their personality and their self-concept.

There are many cases of young people and adolescents who believe they are incapable of doing something positive, since their parents, people who are supposed to love them, have always told them from an early age that they cannot do anything right.

It is convenient to explain to children why it is important for them to do their homework. Children understand and have to some extent the ability to understand simple situations, analyze them and learn from them. By explaining to our children the reasons why they should do or not do certain things, it allows them to come to their senses. This will motivate them to do what they are ordered to do, not because they must obey, but because they will understand that it is the right thing to do.

There is nothing better than teaching them by example. If we order our children to do something and, as parents, we are not orderly with our lives, and we do the opposite of what we are trying to ask them to do or not to do.

With what morals can we reprimand them if we do not set an example? It is not enough to ask them to comply with what we ask of them. Let us first be an example for our children. Remember that: They will not do what we ask them to do, but they will copy what we do.

Involve your children to participate in small decisions. It is necessary to spend time with your children, involve them in every task or responsibility at home, talk to them, listen to them, ask for their opinion so that they feel they are an important part of the family.

IS BEING STRICT IN THE UPBRINGING OF OUR CHILDREN A GOOD THING?

I understand that parents want to be friends with their children, and that's fine. However, what is essential is that we are conscientious, considerate and caring parents, without losing respect for our children.

We can be bested friends and parents at the same time, if our children respect us, feel admiration for us, they will most likely look to us for advice and guidance.

Yes, on the contrary, they do not trust us, we have not taught them discipline, to obey and respect adults. No matter how much we are friends with our children, they will not respect us when it comes to reprimanding them.

First, educate your children with love, respect, and discipline. You must guide them on the right path to forge their character through obedience, good manners, education, courtesy and good manners.

All of this should be based on the highest standards, centered on MORAL VALUES and ETHICAL PRINCIPLES. In this way, as our children grow up with this type of upbringing, they will not only be good people, but they will respect us and we will have earned their friendship.

On the other hand, to be authoritarian and demand that our children obey us without refutation is to act from the opposite pole. Of course, we must be firm, without going to the extremes of becoming authoritarian. It is correct to reprimand our children at the right time, without becoming their executioners.

Everything is like a scale, and it must be balanced. Nothing in excess is good, for example: Being too docile, makes our children lose respect for us; while, on the other hand, being too authoritarian will make our children feel fear rather than respect.

Therefore, a good father learns to be an integral, balanced and fair being. He knows how to be firm when the occasion requires it, without mistreating his children. And he knows when he can be more flexible without going to the extremes of being submissive.

As we have reflected so far, the role of parents is an arduous job in which our children must be properly taught from childhood to comply with the rules of the home, moral precepts, as well as to understand the limits and conditions of doing or avoiding certain situations.

Parents should dedicate quality time to their children, share with them, show them love, affection, care, and protection.

Let us learn to be parents with authority and be flexible at the same time. Let us guide our children with a firm hand, if the occasion requires it, always in a balanced, fair, and understandable way. We can reprimand without mistreating and show love at the same time.

At the same time, we learn to be conscious, attentive, considerate parents who listen to their children, pay attention to their needs, are there when they need it and be their best friend. Without ceasing to be their father figure.

SIMPLE AND EFFECTIVE TIPS FOR RAISING SUCCESSFUL CHILDREN

Let's guide our children in their free time to develop an affinity for art, dance, music, singing, sports, among other hobbies with which they feel identified and that allow them to potentialize their talents.

Childhood is the stage of life from which most memories are preserved, as well as the age at which teachings, values, and experiences that mark adult life are transmitted. Therefore, through art, dance, music, singing or sports, the aim is to develop different artistic, creative or athletic skills in childhood. This allows children to connect with those extracurricular activities with which they feel the most affinity.

What are extracurricular activities?

These are activities that take place outside school hours and are not conceived as part of the dynamics of kindergarten, school or the academic routine of the child, youth, or adolescent.

If our children learn to make the right choices, these activities can contribute to their overall development, in addition to improving their performance in many fundamental aspects of their lives.

Why are extracurricular activities important?

Traditional extracurricular or after-school activities, if well directed, can greatly help to improve interpersonal relationships, encourage motivation and full development in children, youth and adolescents.

According to the activity chosen by our children, it can improve in many areas such as coordination, fine and gross motor skills, memory, creativity, passion, discipline, self-esteem, among others.

It also helps them explore a myriad of interests and aspects of their personality. So, here are some general guidelines to help guide you in selecting an extracurricular activity.

1. It should be adapted to the child's interests or preferences and also to his or her temperament, age, and abilities. Our children are the ones who should decide whether they are interested in doing this or that activity, although parents can encourage, motivate and inspire, it should be the children who finally decide to perform those with which they identify themselves the most. These activities must be satisfactory for the child. It is no use for parents to be genuinely interested in their children doing a particular activity if the child is not inspired by it at all.

2. It is crucial to never force our children to do something if they dislike it. Furthermore, it is good, if the child still does not know what to decide, that their parents encourage them to try different activities for a few days to see which one they like the most. Once the child has had the opportunity to have several alternatives, it is ideal that their parents support them in selecting among the various options so that the child can select the one they enjoy doing the most.

3. Avoid overcrowding. Children need to rest and have time to play freely, and even to "do nothing" in certain periods of time. So as parents, we must give them their time and space, so that our children in their free time can decide what to do by themselves.

Learning and having fun. Never forget that children need both equally.

CHILDREN AND TECHNOLOGY

Times are changing. We live in the age of technology and children have learned to quickly become familiar with cell phones, tablets, computers, video game consoles and other smart devices.

The question many parents ask themselves is: ***What is better for my children, traditional methods, or new technologies?***

DIGITAL TECHNOLOGY VS. TRADITIONAL METHODS, WHICH IS BETTER?

It is necessary to ask ourselves some questions to find the answer: ***Is the link between children and technology good*** *or, on the contrary,* ***are traditional methods better***? ***Should I as a parent bet on classic games and traditional activities*** *or* ***on digital applications?*** The truth is that both tools are totally effective to help the early learning and formation of our children.

The use of technology by children continues to be the subject of debate among certain groups of specialists. However, the reality is that it is not a question of whether technology is good or not.

It is about teaching (educating) our children from an early age to use them in a responsible and safe environment.

There are a myriad of educational applications for children with very beneficial effects on their development. However, the important thing is to find the balance between traditional learning methods and the responsible and controlled use of technology.

It is true that the more traditional methods require time and effort for parents, and we are not going to lie, today's frenetic lifestyle turns this traditional method into a challenge, which is to spend quality time with our children.

That is why, relying on digital technology tools, makes it easier to keep our children entertained at home, from a completely educational and safe environment for them, while they play and learn.

They can do this through a whole range of virtual learning games such as puzzles, songs, memory games, videos, audiobooks, among many other digital tools offered by many mobile applications. And they don't have to do it all by themselves – parents can also spend quality family time doing many of these activities and learning together!

The importance of technology in education

The most important thing about the link between technology and our children is the multiple benefits that these tools offer them. A personalized learning environment can make children feel more motivated to learn and boost their education.

For example, it allows them to let their imaginations run wild in their adventures, discovering new concepts and words as they play. This exploration of the imagination will prepare them for school and academic education in subsequent years.

In conclusion: We can allow our children to use technology, without stopping traditional activities. Since both methods are valuable and each of them benefits our children in one way or another.

Next, I will share with you some other advantages that technology offers in relation to education and early learning.

8 Benefits of technology for education.

1. It's fun and motivating – the more children play, the more they learn! It has been shown in recent studies that babies and toddlers learn more easily if they are having fun.

Games, songs, stories and creative crafts are some activities they can do the most with. In addition, the desire to keep learning will increase!

2. Promotes active learning. The active learning period occurs when the child is benefiting from time spent using an electronic device. For example, if they are acquiring school or academic learning, developing "soft skills", doing physical exercise, exercising problem-solving or improving their memory, all of this is favorable for them.

On the other hand, there is the opposite or counterproductive side, which would be the "passive" screen time that does not benefit at all the development of our children. Such as, for example, spending time watching a series on TV for long periods of time, since this type of program does not allow interaction with the content they consume.

This is where parents come in, and their responsibility to teach their children to use these technologies intelligently. It is about teaching and educating our children from an early age to use these methodologies in a responsible and safe environment. Setting certain rules, such as viewing time, types of digital activities allowed, leisure time for traditional outdoor activities, along with the enjoyment of other extracurricular activities such as art, dance, music, singing, sports, among other hobbies with which they also feel identified and allow them to enhance their talents in a balanced and balanced way.

3. Improve communication skills. Paying attention to the tasks necessary to complete an activity will require children to use their mental listening and speaking skills.

In addition, playing together as parents and children will strengthen family bonds by spending quality time together and practicing communication between the two.

4. Improves retention. Interest in learning improves retention in the brain. This means that technology can be a great help for this, especially in the long term.

5. Encourages individual learning as well as participatory collaboration. Some technological methods can better meet the different needs that each of our children may have. Each of them will be able to progress and learn at their pace, time and space, going back to the topics that are more difficult for them or moving on to the next ones after completing a level.

In addition, it can motivate them to be more collaborative when they are learning together with their friends or family.

6. It teaches them the skills necessary to adapt to the 21st century.

As we have learned so far, digital tools are a great teaching, learning and training methodology with great benefits for our children! Children and technology are the perfect combination for learning the 4 C's: creativity and imagination, critical thinking, collaboration and communication.

7. They are accessible from anywhere. Technology does not require schedules, your children will be able to learn from anywhere in the world, at any time! This is ideal for parents with extended workdays, as they can monitor their children's progress, motivate, and inspire them, without leaving their work responsibilities aside.

8. Online technology together with offline tools. The digital era has no limits! Many of the things that can be done in mobile applications can be done in real time (online) or brought to real life in a simple way. For example, learning to brush your teeth, taking care of the environment, baking a delicious cake or learning a new school skill. All from the safety and comfort of home.

Additional tips for the proper use of technology

Make sure the content your kids use is safe. No ads, kidSAFE certified, and most importantly, that your children's data is protected.

Follow the recommendations of experts, such as the American Association of Pediatrics and Psychiatry.

Limit the time of use. You must teach your children to limit their time, establish limits, always with common sense and dialogizing at all times with your children, to maintain order and proper use.

Agree on rest times, especially during school or academic hours, during meals, during family sharing time and at least two hours before bedtime.

Be a good example for the little ones! Let's also set limits for ourselves and our interaction as a family, as this comes with multiple benefits for the development of our children.

Bet on personalized and age-appropriate content.

AWARENESS WHEN IT COMES TO RAISING OUR CHILDREN

As we have learned from the previous chapters, choosing technological strategies and traditional teaching methodologies to educate our children is vital for their full development.

To know the needs of children is to decide to be present as parents in their lives at every moment of their growth.

The child is an integral human being in full holistic development, and once they learn in a disciplined way, about respect, love, obedience, values and living their lives centered on principles, it will be much easier to correct them through good advice and guidance.

Once your children internalize these teachings with high standards, they will be more responsible, loving and considerate children. This allows us to strengthen the bonds of affection in the spirit of family togetherness, communication and trust.

By doing things together with joy and enjoyment, we will be establishing the guidelines for harmony, peace, tranquility, affection, and closeness among the entire family nucleus.

Keep in mind that saying every day how much we love each other is a way to integrate with love and happiness, with sincerity and loyalty, with admiration and affection. In addition, complementing these words with quality time, mutual interest and family sharing will maintain the union and fraternity between parents and children.

We must help each other, fill our lives with hope and expectations to face the winds of renewal and, thus, put into practice an always positive attitude and with the capacity to permanently overcome the adverse situations that may arise.

Showing at all times sincere attitudes of tenderness, apology and manifesting ourselves in our real spiritual dimension.

PAST TRAUMAS

The conflicts and traumas we suffered as children persist into adulthood. The experiences of our early years determine our entire existence; they are emotional wounds that persist even when we reach adulthood.

At times, we feel like the humiliated, rejected, abandoned, betrayed and frightened child we once were.

Occasionally, we do not know what blocks us emotionally or mentally every time we act in this or that way. In great part, the origin of these traumas or emotional wounds was caused when we were children, through those experiences that we could not heal.

For this reason, parents have to understand that we must be a good example for our children, even in their infancy, to avoid causing harm to the little ones.

Many times there are emotional wounds so deep and painful that they affect our personality, and we even transmit them unintentionally to our children, who will also be parents and adults at some point.

HEALING OUR INNER CHILD

The 5 Emotional Wounds.

I will teach you how to recognize the 5 emotional wounds of childhood to heal them and thus, avoid causing them to our children.

Our childhood is so important that our childhood experiences will determine the quality of our adult life as parents.

Psychology points out 5 emotional wounds from childhood that leave their mark even in adulthood. Knowing them is essential to be able to heal them and prevent our children from suffering them as well.

What are emotional wounds?

The emotional wounds of childhood are a kind of affective injury or trauma that prevents us from leading a full existence in our adulthood. Its mark is so deep that it even makes personal relationships difficult. So much so, that it incapacitates us to face problems with greater ease and resistance. It is a great challenge when it comes to raising our children in a healthy and balanced way.

It is common for almost all adults to have one or more of these emotional wounds, more or less deep. The signs of these psychological wounds are evident in an infinite number of ways: such as, for example.

Anxiety, depression, anger, rage, failure in emotional relationships, obsessive thoughts, greater vulnerability to certain psychological and emotional disorders, sleep difficulties, defensive or aggressive attitude, insecurity, fear, distrust, among others.

Human beings learn to interpret the world around us in our first years of life. Our particular interpretation of reality is influenced by our environment, family, socioeconomic, cultural and educational context.

We all have a past. And even if it no longer exists, the experiences lived in childhood mark our character, leaving their mark on it. So, the question is...

Why do they arise? And what are their causes?

Every so often these wounds are due to a really traumatic childhood past. Other times, on the other hand, they are due to distortions in the child's interpretation of reality.

We must remember here that, since our infancy, which goes from 0 to 7 years old in what we call the adsorption phase, we are perfect at capturing impressions and having sensations. However, being so small, we do not have enough conscious capacity to accept or reject the information we receive.

Young children are still too young to understand what is going on around them. For example: A child may feel neglected when, even though his parents are at home with him, they never pay enough attention to him or neglect his emotional needs.

They may also interpret as abandonment the fact that he is left with the grandparents to go to the hospital for a period of time, when in reality his parents are trying to prevent him from suffering due to, for example, an illness within the family.

How do Emotional Wounds Originate?

The emotional wounds of childhood originate from one or more negative experiences (or interpreted as such) lived in childhood.

These experiences leave an emotional imprint (or wound) that can have repercussions on emotional health when we reach adulthood.

Emotional wounds, on the other hand, originate at an early age and as a result of an event or traumatic experience (or appreciation of it) occurring on a one-time basis or over time and more or less constantly.

For example: the death of a family member, depression of one of the parents, inadequate parenting, abuse, the birth of a sibling and the jealousy associated with it...

Sometimes just a perceived sensation, together with extreme sensitivity or susceptibility, is enough to generate the wound based on a misunderstanding or misinterpretation of reality.

This is because these types of emotional wounds occur in the first stage of life. In those early years of our childhood, in which children still lack an adequate approach to reality, personal strategies to manage and understand certain dimensions or poor management of emotions.

In this way, it is common for one or more of the 5 types of painful experiences or emotional wounds of childhood that most affect the psycho-emotional development of the child to occur. They end up leaving a very evident mark on the child's personality.

Knowing them, knowing how each of these emotional wounds arises and what each one consists of is important to avoid or heal them.

So, let's learn from each of them.

1. FEAR OF ABANDONMENT.

For those who have experienced abandonment in childhood, loneliness is their greatest enemy.

The lack of affection, companionship, protection, care, and love marked them so much in their childhood that they are constantly on guard against being abandoned again, so that now, as adults, they feel an extreme fear of being left alone.

People marked with the wound of abandonment show this lack of affection in their personal and emotional relationships.

In numerous instances, they suffer from emotional dependence and will even tolerate the intolerable in order not to feel or remain alone. In other cases, depending on their personality, they will take the initiative to abandon others as a protection or defense mechanism, for fear of reliving the experience of abandonment once again.

How to heal the wound of abandonment:

The wound of abandonment is healed by working on the fear of loneliness. This is achieved in several ways. For example: Spending quality time with ourselves, doing activities we enjoy, and practicing self-care. In addition to identifying and knowing how to manage the fear of being rejected, it is equally relevant to avoid doing so to other people.

To complete this, we must break down the invisible barriers of physical and emotional contact. And open us to receive and give love. That is, to allow ourselves to love and be loved, without attachments.

It is the inner child, and not the adult, who fears being left behind. For this reason, we must strengthen our self-esteem to avoid falling into self-sabotage. And for this, it is necessary to connect with our inner child and embrace him, giving him love so that he feels safe and is able, little by little, to enjoy his moments of solitude.

How to avoid the wound of abandonment in our children.

The way to avoid the wound of abandonment with our children is to share quality time with them, dialogizing often with them, paying conscious attention to their affective needs and practicing active listening and sharing time.

2. FEAR OF REJECTION.

Fear of rejection is one of the deepest emotional wounds because it implies the rejection of our thoughts, feelings, emotions, and experiences; that is, the rejection of our love and even of our person.

It has its origin in experiences of lack of acceptance by parents and close relatives (grandparents, uncles, aunts, uncles, or siblings). As well as from peers (friends) as the child grows up.

When a child receives signs of rejection, the seed of self-contempt grows inside him. He thinks he is not worthy to love, nor to be loved. So, he internalizes this feeling, interpreting everything that happens to him through the filter of his wound.

Thus, there comes a time when the slightest criticism causes him suffering and, to compensate for it, he needs the recognition and approval of others.

How to heal the wound of rejection.

The wound of rejection is healed by starting to value oneself and to recognize oneself, ignoring the messages that the inner critic sends them.

To heal its scar, it is healthy to work on insecurities, gain more self-confidence and begin, little by little, to feel more capable, confident and determined. It is necessary to know, respect, love and accept oneself.

How to prevent the injury of abandonment in our children.

To prevent this injury, we must always treat our children with respect and instill self-confidence in them. Teaching them to have autonomy in decision-making.

It is also significant to teach them to receive constructive feedback and discard destructive criticism, based on self-esteem. As parents, we can practice, recognize their achievements and encourage them with words of affirmation.

3. THE WOUND OF HUMILIATION.

The wound of humiliation opens up when the child feels that his parents disapprove of him and criticize him all the time, directly affecting his self-esteem.

Especially when they are ridiculed or criticized in public. Such children build a self-dependent personality. They are willing to do anything to feel useful and valid for others, which contributes to further feed their woodenness. For their own self-recognition depends on the image others have of them, and not the image they have of themselves.

Those who have suffered humiliation as children have difficulty expressing themselves as adults, and specialize in ridiculing themselves and others. Sporadically, they consider themselves much smaller, less important and worthy, valuable or capable than they really are.

They are people who tend to forget their needs to please others and gain their affection, approval, and respect.

How to heal the wound of humiliation.

This wound is healed by releasing the heavy burden of the past, which the humiliated person carries on his back. It is achieved through forgiveness towards the people who harmed him and towards himself.

Making peace with the past so that he can begin to value himself as the person he really is in the present, and enjoy the future life he is responsible for shaping as an adult.

How to prevent the wound of humiliation in our children.

Through respectful parenting, the empathetic and affectionate treatment of parents towards their children. In addition to knowing how to set limits with respect and love, never reprimanding or criticizing the child in public will prevent our children from suffering the consequences of humiliation during their childhood and in adulthood.

4. THE WOUND OF BETRAYAL OR THE FEAR OF TRUSTING.

The wound of betrayal or fear of trust arises when the child has felt betrayed by a parent, when the parent has repeatedly failed to keep a promise.

This situation, above all, becomes entrenched in the child if it is repetitive. That is to say that it is a habitual situation for the parents, to offer something, and then never fulfill it.

What these actions will generate in the child are feelings of isolation and distrust. Occasionally, these emotions can turn into resentment *(when the child feels cheated for not having received what was promised)* or envy *(when the child feels deserving of what was promised and other people have it while he/she does not).*

This emotional wound builds a strong, aggressive, possessive, distrustful and controlling personality. The need to be always in control so as not to feel cheated predominates in the person.

They are people who attach great importance to fidelity and loyalty. However, they tend to distort both concepts. They are extremely possessive people, to the point of not respecting the freedom, space, or limits of others, sometimes not even letting them breathe.

How to heal the wound of betrayal and fear of trust.

To heal this wound, we must work on patience, tolerance, trust, and forgiveness. Likewise, we must learn to cultivate the delegation of responsibilities to others, learn to trust and believe in people.

In addition, we must work on forgiveness, close cycles and allow ourselves to trust others, give ourselves a chance to see the best in people. While remaining cautious and overly cautious.

How to prevent the wound of betrayal and the fear of trusting our children.

To avoid it for our children, we must not promise in vain, we must be consistent in our words and actions. Let us learn to always keep the promises we make to them. And in a moment that we fail to fulfill it, reward it later, sincerely.

5. THE WOUND OF INJUSTICE.

The emotional wound of injustice originates when parents are cold and rigid with their children, imposing an authoritarian and disrespectful education on them.

Constant demands and perfectionism will generate in children's feelings of inefficiency, uselessness... and a sense of injustice.

This emotional wound generates rigid adults, who cannot negotiate or hold dialogues with diverse opinions. In addition, they find it difficult to accept other points of view and ways of being different from their own.

They give much more importance to beliefs and not to values, expressing their opinions and moral judgments as absolute and extreme truths, without respecting the point of view of others.

Their intentions usually revolve around gaining power and importance, being fanatical about order and perfectionism.

How to heal the wound of injustice.

The way to heal this wound is to work on mental rigidity, cultivating flexibility, tolerance, and trust towards others.

How to prevent the wound of injustice in our children.

It is prevented from childhood by teaching our children respect for diversity and tolerance, in addition to practicing respectful parenting, social empathy, the expression of feelings and the exchange of opinions and ideas in a healthy and balanced manner.

THE BENEFITS OF PHYSICAL CONTACT

Did you know that giving a sincere hug to our children is very healing, especially when they are sad? This healing effect is multiplied in the little ones and strengthens the bond of love and closeness between the two of you.

Hugging is such a powerful gesture that it not only benefits children, but has the same healing effect on us adults.

Hugging has many benefits for us as parents as well as for our children. For that reason, start hugging the little ones with all your sincere love, it will comfort both of you.

Science has demonstrated the great power of hugs in brain development: Among the most known positive effects is that it allows us to release hormones that produce well-being and reduce stress levels.

Among them, we can highlight dopamine, oxytocin, serotonin, and endorphin. Four powerful hormones that produce what we know as the chemistry of happiness.

There will always be an ideal moment to share this simple and powerful act that brings more benefits than many therapies.

When we receive or give a sincere hug, we feel loved, understood, protected and comforted. In a couple of seconds we recover our emotional balance and feel that all is well.

Benefit of hugging in children.

This is what happens when children feel mom and dad's embrace:

1. Hugs release dopamine, known as the pleasure hormone. Therefore, we will have happier, cheerful, and motivated children. With a great capacity for imagination, intuition, and creativity.

2. Hugging activates skin receptors and kinesthetic stimulation. In a hug, the immediate contact stimulates the skin, acting on the dermis. The pressure

in turn stimulates the vagus nerve, which is responsible for regulating blood pressure.

In other words, we calm stress and regulate blood pressure. With a hug, we calm our body, experiencing a sense of well-being and pleasure.

3. Hugging releases oxytocin, commonly called the love hormone. For this reason, hugs are significant from the birth of a baby and throughout its development, growth, and formation, as this love effect in children is responsible for feelings of trust and security.

4. Hugging reduces the level of cortisone in the blood (cortisol, a hormone known as the stress hormone). Body contact through hugging very pleasant stimulates tactile sensations and generate a state of emotional well-being.

5. Hugs make people happy, whether they are children, youth and adolescents, including adults. Therefore, a hug gives us a sense of emotional strength, improves our self-esteem and, most importantly, fills us with happiness, love, and fraternity.

A hug, although it is such a simple gesture, when it is sincere, is charged with a great emotional energy that makes the people who give and receive it connect energetically.

In conclusion, we can affirm that: Hugging is the most powerful non-verbal expression that parents can give to their children. Therefore, it is recommended to hug daily and constantly.

NINE STEPS TO EFFECTIVE PARENTING

Raising our children is one of the most difficult, yet most satisfying and rewarding tasks in the world. However, it is also a responsibility for which, at times, as parents we may feel that we are not as well-prepared as we had hoped.

Relax, I understand, so below I'll share nine tips for raising children. Tips that can help you feel more prepared as a parent while learning to enjoy raising your children more.

1. Stimulate your child's self-esteem.

Children begin to develop their sense of self from the time they are babies, when they see themselves reflected through their parents' eyes.

Your children assimilate and learn to recognize your tone of voice, your body language and all your body expressions and facial gestures.

For that reason, your words and actions as a parent have a greater impact on the development of a child's self-esteem than anything else.

Sincere praise and recognition of their accomplishments, however small, will make children proud; allowing them to do things on their own, these small actions will make them feel capable and strong. Conversely, belittling comments or negative comparisons to other children will make them feel bad.

So, avoid negative statements or using hurtful words. Comments such as "What a stupid thing to say!" or "You act more like a baby than your little brother!" can cause more harm than physical blows.

So, choose your words carefully and be compassionate. Tell your children that everyone makes mistakes and that you still love them, and even when they will support you, so they can do better next time.

2. Recognize your good deeds.

Have you ever stopped to think about how many times a day you have negative reactions to your children? You may realize that, perhaps, you criticize them many more times than you congratulate them, praise them and recognize their small achievements.

The most positive approach to good parenting is to recognize our children's good deeds, no matter how small they may be: For example, "You made the bed without me asking, that's great!" or "I was watching you while you were playing with your sister, and you were very patient", thank you, your little sister thanks you and so do we.

These comments are much more effective in encouraging good behavior eventually than continual reprimands and disregard for the contributions of younger children.

As a parent, set out to find something positive to praise and acknowledge your children's small actions every day.

Be generous with rewards: Giving your love, hugs and sincere praise can work wonders and are often rewarding enough for children. You will soon discover that you are "cultivating" in your child, to a greater extent, the behavior you would like to see in him or her.

3. Set limits and be consistent with discipline.

Discipline is necessary in every home. The goal of discipline is to help children appropriately choose acceptable behaviors and learn self-control.

They may test the limits you set, but these limits are essential for them to become responsible adults.

In addition, setting rules at home helps children understand your expectations and develop self-control. Some rules may include, for example, not watching television until homework is done, and teaching them never to use hitting, name-calling, or hurtful teasing.

It is recommended that you implement a system. That is, a warning followed by consequences, which can be a penance or the loss of a privilege if they break a rule.

A common mistake parents make is not following through with established consequences. You can't discipline children for a bad action one day and ignore it the next. Being consistent and consistent will teach your children what you expect of them.

4. Make time to share with your children.

It is often difficult for parents and children to get together for a family meal, let alone spend quality time together to strengthen their parent-child bond.

However, there is probably nothing children would like more than that, to feel that you spend time and really care about sharing with them.

Make it a habit to get up 10 minutes earlier in the morning, so you can have breakfast with your children, or you can leave the dishes in the sink and share some quality time with them after dinner.

Children who do not receive the attention they need from their parents regularly inadvertently overreact or misbehave because they will receive their attention, whether they are aware of it or not.

Many parents find that it is rewarding for everyone to schedule time to spend with their children. Schedule a "special night" or "family day" each week to be together, and let your children help decide how to spend that time together.

In addition, you can find other ways to interact with them daily, for example, put a note or something special in the children's lunch boxes, tell them a bedtime story or simply walk them to bed, put them to bed for years and say goodnight with a kiss and a hug.

On the other hand, adolescents appear to need less individual attention from their parents compared to younger children. However, they also require their love, companionship, attention, and care.

Since there are fewer opportunities for parents and their teenagers to spend time together, parents should make every effort to be available when their older children express a desire to talk to them, participate in family activities, or require their advice.

Attending concerts, joining them in sports, participating in school activities and other events with your teen is a great way to show your affection. It also lets you learn other important things about your child and his or her friendships.

Don't feel guilty if you are a working parent. Children will remember the little things you do for them, such as making popcorn, playing videos, playing games with them, watching their sports games, accompanying them somewhere, etc.

5. Be a good role model for your children.

Young children learn a lot about how to act by watching their parents. The younger they are, the more they imitate you.

So, before reacting aggressively or getting angry in front of your child, think about the following, ***Is this how you want the child to behave when angry?***

Always be aware that your children are watching you. Studies have shown that, in general, children who hit are doing so because they are largely imitating the pattern of aggression in their homes.

Set an example of the positive qualities you wish to cultivate in your children, such as: Respect, cordiality, honesty, kindness, service, patience, discipline, love for one's fellow man, among others.

Be generous. Do things for others without expecting retribution in return; your children will see that example in you. Express your appreciation and give sincere praise. Above all, treat your children the same way you expect others to treat you.

6. Make communication a priority in your home.

You can't expect children to do everything you tell them to do, just because you as a parent "say so". They want and deserve explanations, just as adults do, to make the best decisions.

If we don't spend time explaining, children will begin to question their values and motivations, and whether they are well-founded. Parents who reason with their children allow them to understand and learn without making value judgments. This will raise children who are more aware, participative and willing to follow advice.

Make your expectations clear. If there is a problem, describe it, express your feelings sincerely and lovingly, and invite your child to work together as a family to find a solution.

Never forget to mention the consequences. Offer suggestions and offer alternatives. Furthermore, be willing to listen to the suggestions and options for your children may offer. Negotiate with them.

Children who are involved in making decisions are more motivated to carry them out, to keep agreements and keep their word, if they see that their parents also keep their part of the bargain.

7. Be flexible and willing to adapt your parenting style as circumstances change.

If your child's behavior often disappoints you in some way, it may be because your expectations are unrealistic. And they are not in line with your child's age, understanding, expectation or needs.

Remember, each person is different, has his or her style, learns at his or her pace and there are differences between one child and another. So, you can never pretend that what is right for one of your children will be ideal for the other. So, you must adapt to the ages, understanding, expectations or needs of each child separately.

The environment that surrounds children has a great impact on their behavior and way of being; therefore, it can change any behavior if it modifies the environment.

For example: If you continually have to tell your 2-year-old "no" to stay away from a certain place, find some way to restructure the environment so that there is another way for the toddler to get around without breaking the rule. This will be less frustrating for both of you. At the same time, it will strengthen your parent-child bond.

As your child changes and grows, you will gradually have to modify your parenting style. Chances are that what is effective with your child today will not be as effective in a year or two. So adapt to change, be flexible and aware.

Teens tend to look more to others for role models and less to their parents as they get older. However, never stop guiding, modeling and encouraging your teen, and providing appropriate discipline while they are with you. At the same time, allow your children to become more and more independent. And take advantage of every moment you have to build a good relationship.

8. Demonstrate that your love is unconditional.

As a parent, you have a lifelong responsibility to correct and guide your children. However, the way you express your corrective guidance has a great influence on how a child receives it.

When resolving issues with your children, avoid blaming, criticizing or fault-finding, which can weaken self-esteem, destroy confidence and cause resentment.

Instead, try to nurture and encourage with love, even when disciplining your children. Make sure they know that, although you want and expect better next time, your love is unconditional.

9. Be aware of your needs and limitations as a parent.

Face it: You're not a perfect parent. As the head of the household, you have strengths as well as weaknesses. Acknowledge your abilities: "***I'm caring and dedicated.*" *While at the same time*** acknowledge your weaknesses and commit to working on them: ***"I need to be more consistent with discipline."***

Try to have realistic expectations for yourself, your spouse and your children. You don't need to know all the answers: Just be understanding of yourself, improve in the areas you know you need to improve and focus on the areas you know you are good at and acknowledge them.

Try to make parenting a manageable task. Focus on the areas that require the most attention, rather than trying to tackle all challenges at once. Admit when you feel burned out and take your time to move forward.

Focusing on your needs does not make you a selfish person. It simply means that you care about your well-being, another important value for your children to take you as an example to follow. Remember, we all require a moment to ourselves, and to supply our needs, this is something totally natural, normal and above all it is a personal duty of each person.

TIPS FOR RAISING SUCCESSFUL CHILDREN

The debate regarding the education and upbringing of children is more lively than ever lately because we are in a time of transition. A transition in which we are moving from an authoritarian and adult-centric educational style; to a more democratic, more inclusive, and respectful one, which takes more into account the needs and freedoms of children, as well as their motivations.

Now at last, to shed some light on the debate, I will share the latest research on the subject, definitive tips for raising successful children.

1. Make every effort to establish a loving, brotherly and sisterly caring relationship with your children.

According to Harvard psychologists, children learn to be kind and loving to others when they are treated that way.

When our children feel loved, respected and cared for, they have a better relationship with their parents. As a result, they are more receptive to living the values and teachings imparted by their parents within the nuclear family.

To do so, it is necessary to attend to both their physical and emotional needs, providing our children with a stable, affectionate and safe family environment in which we respect their individual personalities, take a real interest in their things and talk about what they consider important.

This is achieved by spending quality time together, even scheduling time for this purpose: For example, in the evenings while telling a story to the younger ones, on Saturday afternoon, finding time exclusively for a particular child, supporting him/her in a school, sports or cultural activity. In other words, doing things that both parent and child enjoy doing together.

In addition, have conversations in which you can elaborate on meaningful things frankly and openly: some examples to highlight would be... What they have learned at school or in their extracurricular activities; if someone has done something nice for them, or if they have felt good doing something good for others. What things have been more difficult for them to understand or deal with lately, and how their parents can help them in a given situation, etc.

2. Get to be a valid example for your children.

Children learn ethical values and moral behaviors by observing the actions of their parents and those of adults whom the children also respect.

To be an example for our children to look up to, we must be aware that we are being honest, fair, and able to resolve conflicts through dialogue, kindness, and justice. As well as being able to manage anger and learn to control other difficult emotions effectively.

Sometimes, perhaps there will be times when as human beings we make mistakes because no one is perfect, the ideal is that we recognize our mistake and try to correct it in the most appropriate way possible. In this way, our children will also learn from that part of our character, which makes mistakes and makes mistakes, and our assertive response to it.

The important thing is to learn to be of integrity and develop the honesty to be able to ask for forgiveness and apologize when the occasion calls for it, and to try to make amends for our failures in a more appropriate way and commit ourselves to never set out to repeat them again.

Children want to be like their parents if they respect them, if they hold them in high esteem or good regard for how they treat them and how they make them feel. On the other hand, a parent who is emotionally distant from their children will hardly be an example that their children will want to follow.

3. Make caring for others a priority and establish high ethical commitments.

It is crucial that children see that their parents care about others and have a desire to serve their fellow man, as children will perceive this principle as something valuable to apply to their personality.

Let children see that the essential thing in life is to be kind and at the same time to be courteous and happy in helping others. Let children be as committed as parents to doing what is right, what is good, what is just, even when other people do not behave that way, nor thank them for the service rendered.

It would be something like learning that what is fair is above individual desires and the recognition of each person; teaching them to seek happiness through kindness, to feel good by making other people happy; giving value to group work, teamwork, and encouraging them to work ethically, towards all those people around them.

4. Help them to be grateful and kind.

When children are kind to others, they are more able to see the gestures of kindness toward them, and in general, the more appreciative they will be.

Studies strongly suggest that people who are more likely to express gratitude tend to be more generous, compassionate and able to forgive, close cycles and move on. They are also more likely to be happier and live healthier lives.

For a child to be kind and grateful, he must simply live in a climate that is consistent with these same principles. In this way, as they grow older, our children will be more able to help others and be grateful for what they do for them; and when they have the opportunity to spend time with other children, if conflict arises, they will have the tools to negotiate and mediate so that differences can be resolved in the best way possible.

If this also happens at home, it allows children to give their opinion when there are disagreements. In this way, they will learn to be fair, to listen, to debate and to solve problems as part of a whole in the family nucleus. In this way, they will also be able to participate in the good functioning of their family, in the way to achieve the happiness of forging a better and warm home for all.

In addition, children should have real responsibilities: They should participate in household chores on a routine basis, without being punished or provoking exaggerated gratitude on our part.

When we simply expect our children to do what they know they have to do and do not reward them for what is their duty, we will be teaching them responsibility and discipline. Of course, when they do unusual acts of kindness, and we recognize their efforts, it is more likely that such actions will become part of their routine and lifestyle.

When children collaborate at home, they are also more capable of appreciating what their parents do for them and what they themselves do for the good of the household.

5. Broaden the children's circle of empathy towards other people.

Children usually empathize with a small circle of family and friends. The challenge for parents is to help them also empathize with those who are not part of their inner circle.

For example, teaching empathy with a new child at school, empathizing with a child who may not yet have mastered communication, or someone who is going through a rough patch and needs a helping hand.

Psychologists consider it important for children to learn to know what is going on with people. From there, to be able to recognize the vulnerability of others, the feelings of those who have problems and offer a helping hand without expecting anything in return.

For example: talking to that child who has just arrived and feels alone, defending a child who is being abused, etc. And it is even essential to teach our children the repercussions that their actions can have on others, both for good and for bad.

6. To promote analytical thinking and action for change.

Children are naturally interested in ethical issues because they are genuinely interested in understanding why things are the way they are, and why some people act the way they do.

Often, when faced with an injustice, children consider taking some action to help, and parents should be able to empower that desire to promote such positive changes in our children.

To complete this, we recommend talking as a family about the different dilemmas that occur throughout the day in the child's life. For example, when a child says negative things about another child, and how he/she responds; when he/she sees someone cheating on a test or stealing, how he/she feels about it; when someone is afraid to admit that he/she was wrong or did something wrong, how the child thinks that person should have reacted; or when someone mistreats an animal, etc.

This type of conversation allows the child to express him/herself freely, and gives parents the opportunity to teach values.

7. Helping our children develop self-control and manage their feelings effectively.

Teaching children that all feelings should be considered appropriate and valid is fundamental to developing healthy emotional intelligence. However, we must also teach our children that the reaction they elicit in certain situations is not always appropriate. In that way, we can teach children to deal with their negative feelings more productively, effectively and efficiently at the right time.

To accomplish this, we must talk a lot about feelings with them, and try to name those feelings when they have them so that they learn to recognize them. For example: "Son, I think you are sad", "I know you are angry", "you feel frustrated because"....

In this way, we encourage them to talk about those feelings, and to try to understand their reaction and response to the situation. In addition, we give them the opportunity to think about what they would like to do and what they may or may not be able to do in such a circumstance.

Even more, to understand why they feel this way and to offer alternatives so that they see that there is no single way to channel emotions, be they anger, rage, frustration, or anger.

In addition, it is advisable to rehearse conflict resolution with them. If we are witnesses of one, or if the child has been one, we can talk about it, to see how he/she would react or respond and express how he/she thinks it should be solved.

Show him how useful it is that both people, the two who are in conflict, can talk and express their feelings, say how they have felt, so that one can understand the anger of the other, to reach a mutual understanding from which the conflict between the parties can be solved.

Finally, I recommend setting clear boundaries for our children, wisely using authority to express what are the logical rules for living together when necessary. I must remind them that these rules are based on sincere and reasonable concern. And that they are communicated out of love for the child's well-being and honoring them and others.

Always focused on the highest standards, based on MORAL VALUES and ETHICAL PRINCIPLES. In this way, as our children grow up with this kind of teachings, they will not only be good people, but they will learn to respect us as parents, they will respect themselves, and they will learn to respect others.

Final Words

In conclusion, parenting is a difficult journey, but by applying the right principles and values, it can be a rewarding experience. By engaging in meaningful conversations with your children, setting boundaries and showing unconditional love, you can help create an environment in which they thrive. As parents, we have the opportunity to guide our children in positive ways that will shape their lives for years to come. We must remember that each child is unique and deserves our utmost respect, patience, and love.

PARTING WORDS

Well, "{(congratulations)}", we have now reached the end of this wonderful guide in its special edition that I wrote with so much dedication for you. It was a long process of training and learning that we went through together in this journey towards your success and personal fulfillment as a parent.

This book was created and designed with you in mind, systematically, as a practical step-by-step instruction manual; with the objective of taking you through a mental process of continuous learning, through a well-prepared and simplified "{(pattern of action)}" to provide you with optimal, effective and permanent results in the upbringing and education of your children.

If you liked this book, "**share it**" **with** your help, we can reach more parents and families. Thank you for your contribution.

It's time to start living.

A wonderful life
Focused on principles.
Remember: take action and
Making things happen
And soon you and I will see each other at the
Peak of excellence

You wish you: your great friend Ylich Tarazona

ABOUT THE AUTHOR

Professional Background: M.Sc. **YLICH TARAZONA** recognized, Psychologist, Gestalt Hypnotherapist, International Speaker and Writer, Author of the Reengineering and Mental Reprogramming Series.

Master Coach with NLP and Trainer in NEUROLINGUISTIC PROGRAMMING. Specialist in Alternative Therapies. Ericksonian Hypnosis, Emotional Freedom Technique (EFT – Tapping) and Energetic Healing.

Considered in the media as one of the most prominent and influential professionals in the field of PERSONAL EXCELLENCE. Destined to exert a legacy in the lives of hundreds of people through his PASSION, ENTHUSIASM, DYNAMISM and PRINCIPAL LEADERSHIP.

C.E.O. Founder of HYPNO REENGINEERING and BIO MENTAL REPROGRAMMING ® A Quantum Leap for the Evolution of the SELF and the Awakening of Consciousness.

One of the ONLINE SYSTEMS dedicated to provide COACHING in the CONSOLIDATION of Competencies and Development of the Maximum Human Potential. Specialized in Coaching, Training, and High-Level Training through the techniques of Ericksonian Hypnosis, Neurolinguistic Programming and Mental Reengineering.

Our methodology is designed to enhance the competencies of the individual through a sequence of sessions and therapies. The objective is to guide the coachee to find the necessary tools that allow them to achieve their Goals. Achieve their Objectives and Consolidate Effective Results of Optimal Performance in a specific field of action (Areas of Excellence).

To obtain significant achievements in a more effective way, we accompany our MENTAL HYPNO REENGINEERING and BIO REPROGRAMMING ® process with Life Coaching Sessions. NLP or

Neurolinguistic Programming Techniques, Mental Reengineering, Ericksonian Hypnotherapy, Emotional Freedom Techniques and Quantum Energetic Healing adapted for this purpose.

Author's Books, Audios, and Conferences

Recognized "author of the [brain reengineering and mental bioprogramming] series of books, e-book sequences and keynote lectures".

Among the most outstanding are "program your mind and determine your future", "heal yourself and free yourself from internal self-sabotage", "the power of change and personal reinvention", "position your personal brand or personal branding", reengineering of thought processes, among others.

Creator of the book The Power of Hypnosis and the Practical Hypnosis Course. Extraordinary series of theoretical-practical courses on self-hypnosis and modern hypnosis, trance and hypnotic phenomena, high-level suggestions and inductions, suggestibility tests, covert tests, convinces, and deepeners of hypnotic states that allow the participant to learn "how to hypnotize, anyone, anytime, anywhere".

Creator of the audiovisual webinar, tele-seminar and master conference [rediscovering your purpose and life mission], [the power of focus] and [free yourself from internal self-sabotage], [how to improve your self-esteem], [redesign yourself and reinvent your life], [the power of goals, strategic planning principles and methodologies to reach and conquer your dreams] among others.

Co-creator of the "NLP Model" and the effective formula "{(E – S.M.A.R.T. – E.R.)}" [for goal setting, action plan and strategic planning principles to achieve and consolidate objectives].

Personal Purpose, Mission, and Vision:

Purpose: To transmit to all my readers the necessary strength and resources that will allow them to move forward, always with confidence and optimism, despite adversity.

Guiding them as their mentor and personal coach to find their life mission through a real opportunity for personal growth that will help them clarify their ideas, establish their goals, and elaborate a well-defined plan of action that allows them to successfully conquer their most desired dreams.

Allowing them to create their own future, writing their life story and forging their destiny through a continuous cycle of tactics and strategies created for that purpose.

Likewise, I wish to help my readers change negative thought patterns and limiting mental structures, teaching them to consolidate their competencies and develop their full human potential.

Mission: To become an instrument in God's hands that will allow me to impact the lives of hundreds, thousands, and millions of people around the world.

To leave a footprint that makes a difference in the lives of the people I teach and bring my message to.

As well as to leave them a legacy that transcends in time. And allows them to evolve in all the transcendental and important aspects of their lives, both personally, spiritually, emotionally, and professionally, academically and financially.

Vision: To bring people hope and an option that allows them to transform their lives for the better, to help them develop that seed of greatness that everyone carries inside.

Motivating them to consolidate, position and expand their maximum human potential to the next level of success.

To help them internalize the right principles that allow them to reinvent themselves, creating a new and improved version of themselves.

Opening new paths for them, opening new opportunities for success, allowing them to lead their lives and find themselves again, on the road to transformation and personal excellence.

"I firmly believe that within each of us lies a seed of greatness and a vast reservoir of unlimited potentialities and competencies that usually lie dormant; waiting to be discovered and developed, to blossom into our outer world. When each one of us awakens that individual potential, we rediscover what is our mission and the purpose that gives meaning to our life, we will open the way to a new conscious awakening to what I call personal reinvention and reengineering"

– M.Sc. Ylich Tarazona.

Other Publications, Special Editions, Mini-Courses and Books Created by the Author

Dear reader, it was a pleasure to have shared with you this time of reading, I hope you have enjoyed to the maximum the information contained in this book that I have so lovingly prepared for you.

Your great friend M.Sc. Ylich Tarazona.

1 -. Program your mind and determine your future – improve your self-esteem, focus your thoughts and conquer everything you set your mind to in life.

Heal yourself and free yourself from self-sabotage – learn to strengthen your inner warrior, balance your energetic channels, control your emotions.

3 -. The power of change and personal reinvention – the art of redesigning your life, reinventing yourself, entrepreneurship, innovation and creating a new and improved version of yourself.

4 -. Discover your purpose and find your destiny – foundations for living a life centered on principles and connected to your vision and mission of purpose.

5 -. Positioning your personal brand – how to make a difference, consolidate and position your personal brand in a competitive market.

6 -. The power of goal setting and objective setting – strategic planning principles to achieve and consolidate your dreams and objectives step by step.

7 -. Mental reengineering and thought redesign – learn how to reprogram your mental processes and generate a personal reinvention.

8 -. Neurolinguistic programming – practical guide to applied NLP – modern methodologies and effective techniques to change your life.

9 -. The power of metaphors and figurative language – stories, parables, metaphors and allegories, powerful persuasive tools in communication.

10 -. The power of hypnosis – theoretical-practical manual for training in hypnosis, and the development of persuasive hypnotic skills.

11 -. Practical hypnosis course – how to hypnotize anyone, anytime, anywhere.

12 -. Multilevel marketing networks – the master cycles of duplication and multiplication in network marketing.

13 -. Business planning notebook – monthly action plan to successfully develop your multilevel business professionally.

14 -. Multilevel network marketing – network marketing, the great business opportunity of the XXI century, towards your financial freedom.

15 -. Inspirational words and quotes – collection of over 800 motivational thoughts and quotes from history's greatest leaders.

16 -. Engram and neural consciousness – theory of the relationship between the conscious and subconscious mind.

17 -. The unlimited power of the subconscious mind – take control of your thoughts and program your mind for success.

Hypno-reengineering and mental bio-reprogramming for success – a quantum leap for the evolution of being – the new era of thought and the awakening of consciousness.

19 -. NLP life coaching training – knowledge, skills, techniques, practices, and methodologies of coaching for goal achievement.

*Always keep in mind that: constant learning, continuous training and permanent study are the keys between those who achieve success and those who do not, **M.Sc. Ylich Tarazona.***

You can contact me directly through my website:
https://mscylichtarazona.com/

COPYRIGHT STATEMENT

FIN

Don't miss out!

Visit the website below and you can sign up to receive emails whenever Ylich Tarazona publishes a new book. There's no charge and no obligation.

https://books2read.com/r/B-A-PAIU-URJFC

BOOKS 2 READ

Connecting independent readers to independent writers.

Did you love *Successful Sons Psychotherapeutic Guide for Parents*? Then you should read *Discover Your Life Purpose*[1] by M.Sc. Ylich Tarazona!

[2]

Discover Your Life Purpose

Foundations for living a principle-centered life connected to your vision and mission of purpose

Extraordinary book of self-help, motivation, and self-improvement that will help you rediscover your purpose and life mission in a fantastic journey of personal rediscovery.

Intrapersonal journey that allows you to connect with your inner being and synchronize with your divine destiny.

Allowing you to become the best version of yourself and develop the maximum of your human potential.

Taking your innate gifts, talents, and abilities to the next level, inspiring you to live a principle-centered life.

In this book in its special edition, you will learn to:

---

1. https://books2read.com/u/mBveNk

2. https://books2read.com/u/mBveNk

Discover what your true mission in life is, find your destiny and understand what is the purpose that gives meaning to your existence.Allow you to program your conscious and subconscious mind for success and personal fulfillment. Motivating and inspiring you to fulfill your most desired dreams, goals, and objectives.Synchronize with your destiny, connecting with your vision, mission, and life purpose. Discovering what you are passionate about and what you love to do.Having an action plan and a well-defined step-by-step life project that will help you rediscover your gifts and talents.Develop the maximum of your human potential to a new level of superior consciousness that connects you with the universal energy source.Master the basic principles of personal redesign and reinvention that allow you to transform into the person you want to become and start living an extraordinary life centered on your values.

7th special edition revised, updated and extended

(Includes practical exercises and action plan)

M.Sc. ***YLICH TARAZONA***

Writer and International Speaker

Read more at https://ylichtarazona.com.es/.

Also by Ylich Tarazona

Principes de base du succès et lois préliminaires du succès
Reprogrammez votre esprit et déterminez votre destin

Principi di base per il successo e leggi preliminari del successo
Riprogramma la tua mente e determina il tuo destino

Princípios Básicos para o Sucesso e Leis Preliminares do Sucesso
Reprograme a sua mente e determine o seu destino

Principios Básicos para Triunfar y Leyes Preliminares del Éxito
¡Guía de Autoayuda y Superación Personal!

Principios Psicoterapéuticos para Triunfar y ser Feliz
Hijos Triunfadores - Guía Psicoterapéutica para Padres

Psychotherapeutic Principles for Success and Happiness
Successful Sons Psychotherapeutic Guide for Parents

Reengineering and Mental Reprogramming

Personal Reinvention

Reprogram Your Mind and Determine Your Destiny

The Power to Heal Yourself

Discover Your Life Purpose

The Power of Goals

How to Build Your Personal Brand

Reingeniería y Reprogramación Mental

Reinvención Personal. El Arte de Rediseñar tú Vida

El Poder de Sanarte a Ti Mismo

Descubre Tu Propósito de Vida

El Poder De Las Metas

Cómo Construir Tu Marca Personal

Reprograma Tu Mente y Determina Tu Destino

Watch for more at https://ylichtarazona.com.es/.

About the Author

YLICH TARAZONA reconocido, Psicólogo, Hipnoterapeuta Gestalt, Conferencista Internacional y Escritor, Autor de la Serie Reingeniería y Reprogramación Mental.

Máster Coach con PNL y Trainer en PROGRAMACIÓN NEUROLINGÜÍSTICA. Especialista en Terapias Alternativas. Hipnosis Ericksoniana, Técnica de Liberación Emocional (EFT - Tapping), Sanación Energética, Biodescodificación y Medicina Germánica.

Considerado en los distintos medios de comunicación como uno de los profesionales más destacado e influyente dentro del campo de la EXCELENCIA PERSONAL. Destinado a ejercer un legado en la vida de cientos de personas a través de su PASIÓN, ENTUSIASMO, DINAMISMO y LIDERAZGO centrado en principios.

C.E.O. Fundador de HIPNO REINGENIERÍA y BIO REPROGRAMACIÓN MENTAL® Un Salto Cuántica para la Evolución del SER y el Despertar de la Consciencia.

Uno de los SISTEMAS ONLINE dedicado a brindar COACHING en la CONSOLIDACIÓN de Competencias y Desarrollo del Máximo Potencial Humano. Especializados en el Entrenamiento, Formación y Adiestramiento de alto nivel a través de las técnicas de la Hipnosis Ericksoniana, la Programación Neurolingüística y la Reingeniería Mental.

Nuestra metodología está diseñada para potenciar las competencias del individuo por medio de una secuencia de sesiones y terapias. Que tienen como objetivo guiar a los coachee a encontrar las herramientas necesarias que les permitan Alcanzar sus Metas. Concretar sus Objetivos y Consolidar Resultados Eficaces de Óptimo Desempeño en un campo de acción específico (Áreas de Excelencia).

Con el objetivo de obtener logros significativos de manera más efectiva, acompañamos nuestro proceso de HIPNO REINGENIERÍA y BIO REPROGRAMACIÓN MENTAL ® con Sesiones de Life Coaching. Técnicas de PNL o Programación Neurolingüística, Reingeniería Mental, Hipnoterapia Ericksoniana, Técnicas de Liberación Emocional y Sanación Energética Cuántica adaptadas para tal fin.

Read more at https://ylichtarazona.com.es/.

About the Publisher

YLICH TARAZONA reconocido, Psicólogo, Hipnoterapeuta Gestalt, Conferencista Internacional y Escritor, Autor de la Serie Reingeniería y Reprogramación Mental.

Máster Coach con PNL y Trainer en PROGRAMACIÓN NEUROLINGÜÍSTICA. Especialista en Terapias Alternativas. Hipnosis Ericksoniana, Técnica de Liberación Emocional (EFT - Tapping), Sanación Energética, Biodescodificación y Medicina Germánica.

Considerado en los distintos medios de comunicación como uno de los profesionales más destacado e influyente dentro del campo de la EXCELENCIA PERSONAL. Destinado a ejercer un legado en la vida de cientos de personas a través de su PASIÓN, ENTUSIASMO, DINAMISMO y LIDERAZGO centrado en principios.

C.E.O. Fundador de HIPNO REINGENIERÍA y BIO REPROGRAMACIÓN MENTAL® Un Salto Cuántica para la Evolución del SER y el Despertar de la Consciencia.

Uno de los SISTEMAS ONLINE dedicado a brindar COACHING en la CONSOLIDACIÓN de Competencias y Desarrollo del Máximo Potencial Humano. Especializados en el Entrenamiento, Formación y Adiestramiento de alto nivel a través de las técnicas de la Hipnosis Ericksoniana, la Programación Neurolingüística y la Reingeniería Mental.

Nuestra metodología está diseñada para potenciar las competencias del individuo por medio de una secuencia de sesiones y terapias. Que tienen como objetivo guiar a los coachee a encontrar las herramientas necesarias que les permitan Alcanzar sus Metas. Concretar sus Objetivos y Consolidar Resultados Eficaces de Óptimo Desempeño en un campo de acción específico (Áreas de Excelencia).

Con el objetivo de obtener logros significativos de manera más efectiva, acompañamos nuestro proceso de HIPNO REINGENIERÍA y BIO REPROGRAMACIÓN MENTAL® con Sesiones de Life Coaching. Técnicas de PNL o Programación Neurolingüística, Reingeniería Mental, Hipnoterapia Ericksoniana, Técnicas de Liberación Emocional y Sanación Energética Cuántica adaptadas para tal fin.

www.ingramcontent.com/pod-product-compliance
Lightning Source LLC
LaVergne TN
LVHW022108200926
848481LV00003B/1108
* 9 7 9 8 2 1 5 6 3 7 2 3 4 *